TRIXIE&KATYA'S

Guide to Modern Womanhood

TRIXIE&KATYA'S

Guide to Modern Womanhood

TRIXIE MATTEL

AND

KATYA ZAMOLODCHIKOVA

PLUME

PLUME

An imprint of Penguin Random House LLC

penguinrandomhouse.com

Plume is a registered trademark and its colophon is a trademark of Penguin Random House LLC.

Photos on pages 12–29 and 32–35 by Gabriel D. Gastelum
Photo on page 41 by Joel Benjamin

All other photos by Albert Sanchez with creative director Pedro Zalba

LIBRARY OF CONGRESS CATALOGING-IN-PUBLICATION DATA
Names: Mattel, Trixie, author. | McCook, Brian, 1982- author.
Title: Trixie and Katya's guide to modern womanhood / Trixie Mattel and
    Katya Zamolodchikova.
Description: New York : Plume, [2020] | Identifiers: LCCN 2019051047 (print) |
LCCN 2019051048 (ebook) | ISBN
    9780593086704 (POB) | ISBN 9780593086711 (ebook)
Subjects: LCSH: Women—Conduct of life—Humor. | Beauty, Personal—Humor.
Classification: LCC PN6231.W6 M38 2020 (print) | LCC PN6231.W6 (ebook) |
    DDC 818/.602—dc23
LC record available at https://lccn.loc.gov/2019051047
LC ebook record available at https://lccn.loc.gov/2019051048

Printed in the United States of America
10 9 8 7 6 5 4

Book design by Lorie Pagnozzi

For all the ambitious female
scientists out there

CONTENTS

Introduction: You as a Human Person 1

PART ONE

BEAUTY AND STYLE 9

Hair: Hair Today, Gone Tomorrow 13

Makeup: Beat It! 21

Heels: Using Your Platform for Good! 31

Personal Style: Who the Fuck Are You?! 37

Personal Hygiene: Whoops, I'm Disgusting! 59

Alochol (sorry, i've been drinking) 69

Pills, Pipes, and Potions: Over the Rainbow
and Under the Influence 77

Self-Love: Autoerotic Appreciation 89

PART TWO

HOMEMAKING 101

Money: Are You a Poor? 105

Yes, I'm Perfect: Curating Your Digital Facade 111

Interior Design: Show Me Your Insides 119

Food: The Food Pyramid Scheme 123

Travel: Wherever You Go, There You Are 129

Decluttering Your Condo, Marie 149

PART THREE

RELATIONSHIPS 155

Meeting People: Charmed, I'm Sure 159

Hookups: How to Have Sex with Strangers 165

Breakups: It's Not Me, It's You 171

Friendships: Best Friends Forever 175

Acknowledgments 196

TRIXIE & KATYA'S

Guide to Modern Womanhood

INTRO

DUCTION

YOU AS A
HUMAN PERSON

As far as we know, there are THREE facets of your humanity that make you YOU.

INTELLIGENCE

Have you ever heard the phrase "she's got a good head on her shoulders"? This isn't alluding to your competitively priced dandruff-controlling shampoo. Among all the attributes one can present, being the sharpest acrylic toenail on the foot is the most select. In the real world, outwitting another is the equivalent of creeping up to their ear and whispering, "I am inherently better than you."

The iconic John Waters said, "If you go home with somebody, and they don't have books, don't fuck 'em! Don't sleep with people who don't read!" Truthfully, you don't know where they keep their books, so this advice is fairly incomplete. In the summer, I keep my books in my refrigerator next to my AAA batteries and my watermelon SKYY vodka. Also: *Owning* books doesn't make someone intelligent. *Reading* books doesn't even make someone intelligent. You're reading a book right now and you're dumb as hell.

Of course, intelligence presents in many forms. I once worked the front desk at a prestigious salon in Wisconsin. (Contradictory, I know.) That's where I met Tara, a gorgeous young stylist with glowing skin, bright eyes, and supernaturally blond hair. She had a baby-doll voice and long charcoal lashes. Her clients consisted of women who wanted to be her and married men who wanted to abandon their families and abduct her. I was *obsessed* with Tara.

The average person would look at a "Tara" and decide she couldn't be a thinker. After her client consults, however, I would watch Tara bubble into the color room, pull out her glasses, and transition into a talented chemist. She could double-, triple-process colors and buzz out a couple ultraprecise men's cuts in between. After performing dazzling feats of beauty, she would leave every client feeling like they just had lunch with a Playboy Bunny.

Tara the not-so-scatterbrained stylist can teach us something! I learned that the girl who presents as "ditzy" might not want you to know how smart she is. Wielding intelligence welcomes expectation. It's better to lie in wait as a drooling stooge. Then you can floor everyone by solving a Rubik's Cube at a holiday party and be like, "What?"

BEAUTY

As long as I've been alive, I have known I was gorgeous. The longing glances from adult strangers, the catty remarks from peers, the sexual advances from Uber drivers. Using vocabulary from my Friday afternoon Lyft trip with Mohammad, I am what you would consider "five stars."

However, beauty is entirely in the eye of the beholder. For example: A Trixie Mattel show was reviewed in Newcastle. Let's call the reviewer Kate because that's her name. Kate described me as someone who "revels in the repulsion she exudes." Kate is, as my eye beholds, an ugly fucking cunt.

Of course, many physical attributes are inherently beautiful. Symmetrical features, an oval face, a gold grill. But in modern beauty, individuality and confidence are the oval face. Look at me, for example. Young? Childlike. Tight? As a drum. But I am, most importantly, odd-looking. Some would say I look like Patrick Stewart as a gay farmer. Some would say I look like an ASL interpreter who moonlights as a Klan member. I think I look like Caillou with fetal alcohol syndrome. But looking like a cross-dressing Elmer Fudd gives me uniqueness, and uniqueness has a magnetism all its own. Even now, you are flipping to the cover of this book to reexperience my hypnotizing gaze. Go ahead. I'll wait.

Conversely, let me tell you about my sister. In order to protect her identity, I don't want to use her real name, so let's call her "an embarrassment to my whole family." My sister is classically beautiful. She's a tall Native American goddess. Almond eyes, full cheekbones, and artisanal arched brows. Even our family's tradition of poorly-cared-for teeth (see the chapter titled "Personal Hygiene") hasn't stunted her maturation into what rappers would call a "thicc shawty."

However, the ETMWF has a tongue piercing. She also vapes and makes Instagram videos blowing the smoke out through her nose. A corrupted natural beauty, she is a Westin presenting as an airport Howard Johnson and I cry every night about it. Maybe living in the shadow of my beauty and fame has impaired her.

In any case, a true beauty knows how to make it work, Tim Gunn style. With the transformative magic of styling, hair, and makeup, two gay men can meet on a reality TV competition show and rise to the top of the entertainment industry. Or, for even more of a stretch, you could love yourself.

PERSONALITY

I believe it was the great prophet Britney Jean Spears who said, "There's only two types of people in the world; the ones that entertain and the ones that observe." Beauty is a lovely thing to possess, like dual citizenship or a will to live. And intelligence can really help you own a room—particularly if that room is a commercialized escape-room experience. But a great personality can perform wonders: get an ugly girl invited to a social event, keep Ted Bundy on the run, or even land you and your vascular friend a book deal.

Personality is the characteristic behaviors, patterns, and qualities unique to you. If your beauty is the candy-bar wrapper, your personality is the brick of creamy nougat that says, "I'm fun!"

If you're not sexy, think of personality as a diversion. Who could stay focused on your pockmarked skin when you've got such an innate sense of whimsy? "Is half of her body burned? Oh, never mind—she just did a funny voice!"

Of course, most of our personalities could use a little full-coverage concealer dabbed under the eyes. Maybe pull back on that embarrassing laugh. Save your unpopular political views for that midnight cross burning on your lawn. And most importantly, don't TELL people what to like about you; let people find out what they love about you *on their own.* You are a *Wheel of Fortune* puzzle that you must let those worthy of you figure out *on their own*. Regard your favorable personality traits the way you would feign surprise when complimented on a stunning evening gown—"Oh, this old thing?"

IN CONCLUSION

Of course there's more to your being yourself than intellect, looks, and persona. There are friendships, family, and love . . . but there are also more important components, like your hairdo and the timbre of your voice. All of the facets that make up you as a human person.

In this book, two of America's most beloved model/actresses will guide you through every pivot point of female development, and we will buff out your dry cuticles along the way. Everything you've done, we have done well, and done it with fuller lashes. We have inhabited every reach of your failures, and done it with puke on our uncomfortable shoes.

And may the best woman WIN!

BEAUTY
ST

PART ONE

AND
YLE

HAIR

HAIR TODAY, GONE TOMORROW

by
KATYA

WHAT HAIRSTYLE IS RIGHT FOR YOU?
(SPOILER ALERT: MOST OF THEM ARE BANGS)

SHOULD I GET BANGS?

—HAMLET

There is perhaps no detail as important to the identity of the modern woman as her hairstyle. If you've been anywhere near a television sometime during the last twenty-five years, then all I have to do is say "the Rachel," and you'll instantly know that I'm not referring to the recently acquired midsize sailboat whose dazzlingly vivid airbrushed portrait of celebrity chef Rachael Ray caused quite the stir in Nantucket this summer, but rather the iconic hairstyle sported by Jennifer Aniston in the sitcom *Friends*! The depth and breadth of the Rachel's cultural impact cannot be overstated, as it swept through the chairs of every salon in America and around the world, and its legacy endures today as trend after trend is tested and tossed out by an increasingly fickle public.

Was it a carefully designed strategic endeavor, or was this simple, face-framing, bouncy shag the product of happenstance? According to celebrity hairstylist Jean-Baptiste de MonteCristo, the hairdo was inspired by an Avon saleswoman who was murdered in broad daylight in his hometown. He spent an entire week haunted by the image of her bubbly backlit silhouette until he decided to transfer the negative energy onto Ms. Aniston's head—and the rest is history.

The Rachel quickly spawned a legion of counterfeit, wannabe styles like the much fuller "Raquel," the slicked and sleek "Ray-Gel," and the hot-dog-nacho, ten-minute-dinner-do companion coif "the Rachael," all of which swiftly vanished in the wake of what would become the hairstyling world's undisputed heir to the throne of iconic mononymous cuts: "the Karen," which was actually just the Rachael but with a scrunchie (worn on the wrist).

Though Hollywood stars and their high-paid stylists frantically attempt to create and cash in on the next big trend, it's evident that a truly groundbreaking signature style achieving icon status requires more dumb luck than calculation. As the need to brand and market oneself becomes more and more essential, stars and socialites are going to any lengths to stand out and make a name for themselves. For example, many critics blame the failure of Meg Ryan's career renaissance on a very ambitious and widely mocked attempt at reclaiming the sixties mushroom cut by adding a twenty-four-inch rattail. The tabloids and chat shows wasted no time in mercilessly flogging her as out of touch, insane, unhinged, and "unbelievably fat," while she limped back into obscurity to regroup and try again.

None of this has stifled John Q. Public's and Barbara Regular's botched attempts at branding length, volume, shape, and tone—some of the key ingredients in the recipe for that elusive, truly outstanding, and award-winning coiffure casserole. Scientists have estimated that the average woman age eighteen to forty will spend approximately six hours of each day in a state of mild to severe anxiety about what to do with her hair. From face-framing layers to frosted tips, from bangs to *balayage,* ordinary women across the globe are plagued by the stress of seemingly innocuous personal style queries, such as, "Do blondes really have more fun? And if so, what's the fun differential on color temperature? Do yellow blondes have more or less fun than cool-platinum ash blondes? And will this fun protect me at all against split ends and breakage? Can I just take a shortcut and put on a blond wig? Is being a slut an essential feature of having more fun? Isn't that the clear subtext here, like, blondes are thought to be more desirable and more promiscuous, basically a guaranteed sure thing to all the men in the vicinity? What if I keep my brunette bob and just skip wearing panties?" And so on.

In short, it's a war zone out there, and by "there" I'm talking about the battlefield of the woman's head. . . .

THE NATURAL LOOK

I once lived with a fifty-year-old woman named Gloria who covered her large driveway with oriental rugs. They were in various states of decomposition, stained and tattered by the New England weather, and, of course, trod upon daily by her minivan. When I asked her about the rugs, she just gave me a confused look and changed the subject, choosing instead to direct my attention toward the large bramble she had built in her garden. I looked over at the enormous pile of sticks, branches, twigs, and other foresty detritus and thought, "She paid someone to do this," and wondered why.

She explained that it provided a safe little ground-level hangout for local birds, where they could let their guard down, come chill and squawk, and not have to worry about predators. She was also such an area herself, it seemed, as a flightless pet parakeet often perched on her shoulder. The bird would prune her eyebrows and scream at anyone who approached. It also always left a steady trail of bird shit cascading down her blouse, like a string of antique pearls that grew in size throughout the day.

I thought, "This woman is bizarre, but, more importantly, she is also totally chic," and she inspires me to this day in all areas of my life. So, if you're

looking to take that messy-bun-and-boyfriend-jeans look to the next level, consider upgrading your unkempt rat's nest of a hair-don't into a bohemian bramble hair-do. It might not be the most practical hairstyle or, really, very flattering, and it's certainly wildly inappropriate in most scenarios, but what better feminist rule breaker is there to model your style after than Mother Nature herself? So go ahead and give those long-suffering birds of prey in your neighborhood some much-needed shelter.

FRINGE BENEFITS

There inevitably comes a time in the life of every young woman when she must face her most paralyzing fears, doubts, and insecurities and summon the courage to ask herself one of life's most important questions: Should I get bangs? As a hair and beauty expert I am here to tell you that such crippling quandaries are now unnecessary because the answer is always a resounding yes.

But here's the twist: We no longer have to bear the burden of a bad decision, thanks to the technological innovation known as the clip-on bang. Gone are the days of impulsively hacking into your lusciously long glossy mane to reveal an uneven chunk of jagged fringe sticking straight off your forehead. Modern medicine and the industrial revolution have teamed up to allow any long-haired lady to explore and experiment without the devastating consequences that have forced so many women of previous generations into the convent to grow out their follicular failures in private. Let's take a look at some of these fringe benefits and figure out what they may say about you.

LONG AND LAYERED

Perhaps you are getting older and are unable to afford expensive Botox treatments to smooth out those ever-deepening lines and wrinkles on your forehead. Or maybe you are somehow unwilling to inject nerve-paralyzing toxic chemicals into your face for the sake of vanity. Or, more likely, is there a large hideous scar of a Celtic rune carved into your forehead by the deranged leader of a neo-pagan cult that you've recently escaped that you just don't want to talk about anymore? Did you just burn your eyebrows clean off your face while cooking dinner? Either way, it's time to live out loud and celebrate getting long in the tooth and free in the spirit with an extralong bang that conceals nearly 75 percent of your face. Available in any color under the sun, these lightweight hairpieces can fit in your pocket, conceal any flaw, and be glued right to your head. Wow!

SHORT AND BLUNT

Are you an edgy young woman who rides a bicycle, writes poetry, and carries a large thermos of soup to the movies? Well, turn down the music on your thick, corded headphones, because I've got something to say: Life is short and so are your bangs, and I couldn't be more proud of you for doing something different, unique, a little ugly, and definitely weird, but, hey, if that's the kind of girl you are, I couldn't be more thrilled. You're the kind of girl who looks fear in the face and says, "HUH?!?!?!?!" and then wiggles away coquettishly to arrive late for her shift at the vintage store. You also love wearing glasses, and you should, because they look superb perched right underneath those short, powerful bangs, which act as a sturdy and reliable welcome mat to the dome of your skull.

CAN I SPEAK TO THE MANAGER?

Life is short and so is your patience, which is clearly evident by your pursed lips, your tensed musculature, and, most of all, your no-bullshit hairstyle. When the assistant manager finally makes her way over to the customer service desk, she'll know immediately what she's in for thanks to this severe, shellacked coif that speaks volumes without saying a single word. No need to argue here, even though the return policy is clearly spelled out in bold, plain English on prominently displayed signage throughout the entire store, as well as at the top and bottom of the receipt you've lost, but it's not your fault—your face and hairstyle will get the message across loud and clear, and that message is threefold: (1) You *will* allow me to return this damaged mountain bike that was stolen by my kleptomaniac stepson; (2) I do not care that this is a plus-size women's clothing store; and (3) yes, thank you—I'll take the refund in cash.

MAKEUP: BEAT IT!

A LADIES' GUIDE TO MAKEUP

by TRIXIE

If my house caught on fire (and, honey, with this Beverly Grove 1930s wiring, ticktock, honestly), I would grab three things: a Red Bull, my still-in-the-box 1971 Malibu Barbie, and my makeup bag. In or out of drag, I love to invoke the smoke and mirrors of cosmeceuticals. If I'm going to tell my harrowing tale of escape to the 911 first responders, I'm not going to do it with tired eyes.

The truth is, makeup is daunting. In a world where women are expected to present as eleven-and-a-half-inch teen-model fashion dolls, it is also somehow gauche and discouraged to ask questions about the beautification process. Everyone is just supposed to magically *know.* When I worked at a makeup counter, I always found women *embarrassed.* Their own makeup bags disarmed and intimidated them like one of Jigsaw's brutal traps in the popular horror film series *Saw.* Unless your makeup bag is a Ziploc of anthrax, nothing in there should scare you.

The Mirror Has Two Faces: Who Are You?

In theater school, I was taught that makeup is a way of characterizing yourself before you even speak. From the face paint alone, an audience can deduce so much: Is she old or young? Conservative or daring? Healthy or sick? Glamorous or dressed down? Is she a Bostonian man named Brian who can do the splits?

When you put your makeup on, you're deciding less about how the world sees you and more about how you see yourself. Sounds a little daytime TV, but it's true. I can barely walk in heels until I am in drag. In short, makeup doesn't change people's minds. It changes *our* minds and makes it possible for us to project who we are that day.

When I created my look, these are the icons I threw into my creative blender:

- Audrey from *Little Shop of Horrors*

- Miss Yvonne from *Pee-wee's Playhouse*

- Peggy from *Married . . . with Children*

- Dolly Parton

- Dusty Springfield

- Barbie and Skipper

- Polly Pocket

- My Little Pony

- The Powerpuff Girls

- Lady Bunny

- Amanda Lepore

- Baby Spice

- Hedwig

- Elvira

- Divine

With any look I do, you can usually identify a few borrowed features from these icons. For you, a more boring but still deserving-of-life human being, you can assemble a dream team of your own. Ask an adult to help you cut out some photos from *Woman's Day*. Tack them up near your vanity as a fun little shrine where you can worship.

PRO TIP: Don't burn the place down.

FOUNDATION

The skin is your largest organ (unless you are my second boyfriend, Matthew—woof!). Most people approach skin makeup incorrectly. For most of us, we should not be smearing grout over subway tile. Truthfully, your skin needs less makeup than you think. Unless you're a drag queen—in that case, grab a trowel and try to stop crying backstage for a second while you spackle on, Leslie.

Skin makeup is a forever-changing love story. As a beauty enthusiast, I am always on the hunt for the next newest, coolest thing. Technology is always building on itself, making older formulas become obsolete. I bet in the year 2060 young gays and their fun female friends will read this section and think, "Concealer! These fags were so primitive." These future people will then pop a vitamin, turning their skin an attractive shade of Tiffany blue as they jet-pack out the window to the office. (Ladies and gentlemen, welcome to the stage Tiffany Blue!)

I'm always looking for my new magic potion of skin care/foundation/concealer—the skin base I've always dreamed of—my "make-a-wish foundation," if you will. When I worked in cosmetics, I found that people were more interested in skin camouflage than skin care. That's like stockpiling the morning-after pill instead of pursuing contraception. After enough trips down the stairs in the family room after a missed period, you start to realize that an uncomfortable chat with Mom could have kept your feet on the ground—and your ankles in the air!

At the cosmetics counter, foundation was what we called a "loyalty product," meaning that if someone finds a good formula and shade, they'll remain a loyal consumer. This is because skin makeup is seriously specific. The right mind-set is to match what you *want* to look like with what you realistically can achieve and with what you have to start with.

For me, Tracy Martel, I wear Dermablend Flawless Creator Foundation Drops mixed with MAC Studio Fix Fluid. I get the insane coverage of Dermablend plus the warmth and smooth finish of MAC Fluid. MAC Studio Fix Fluid also photographs like OMGGGG.

Out of drag, I wear MAC Face and Body with Tarte Shape Tape Concealer or Jeffree Star Magic Star Concealer. No one ever knows I have makeup on and both formulas are extremely hydrating.

POWDER

Every time I hear the phrase "set it and forget it," I want to throw up. But truthfully, you'll get more miles out of your makeup with powder. I flour my whole head like a Cornish game hen, but you probably aren't as ugly as me. A light dusting pressed into the skin will keep the children mesmerized by your porcelain surface. I also know drag queens who hide cocaine in their setting powder, so there's that. I personally keep my narcotics away from my complexion products, but I'm old-fashioned.

> THE RIGHT MINDSET IS TO MATCH WHAT YOU *WANT* TO LOOK LIKE WITH WHAT YOU REALISTICALLY CAN ACHIEVE AND WITH WHAT YOU HAVE TO START WITH.

BLUSH

If I had to pick a favorite piece of makeup application, it would be blush. People are just animals. When ovulating, women tend to have more flushed cheeks. So naturally, our eyes find a lively cheek color attractive. I remember as a child picking up my grandma's CoverGirl Cheekers blush, smelling the weird chemical smell, and falling in love. I wore blush full-time as a child and I think everyone assumed I had unaddressed rosacea. (Ladies and gentlemen, welcome to the stage Unaddressed Rosacea!) Or maybe people thought I was a young woman ovulating.

I could opine on blush application styles for each face shape, but I didn't drop out of beauty school to do *Drag Race* so I could become a rule follower. Just know that too little blush will upset me, but too much blush makes you look like you just ran from the police. If I could describe my blush style in one word, I would choose "incriminating." If you look like you've been cooked by a George Foreman Grill, you're Jeffree Star in 2007 and you've gone too far. Reenter the workroom and try again.

MASCARA

From high-end to CVS impulse aisle, with mascara the goal is to always look like one of those baby dolls whose eyes close when you lay her down to sleep. A full lash tells the men of the church, "I am a young person who is gifted genetically. I also have eyes free of debris." Brown-black and black mascara are approved, but if there's one thing I hate, it's colored mascara. Don't fucking come at me with your blue lashes. That's too clownish—even for me!

PRO TIP:
If you've ever applied too much powder blush, liberally veil the area in setting powder and brush off. The powder will carry away the extra blush!

PRO TIP:
With cream blush, apply before foundation for the ultimate natural-woman fantasy.

👁 LASHES

What you want from mascara you can get more of with false eyelashes. I wear eight strips on the top and two strips on the bottom. That's twenty lash strips at once. That's practically one bald goat. If I can wear a farm animal on my upper eyelid, you can at least give the children a little Ardell Demi Wispie. (Ladies and gentlemen, welcome to the stage Demi Wispie!)

👄 LIP COLOR

In times of economic downturn and political strife, lipstick sales take off like a bullet (get it?). Why? Because when people need a little pick-me-up, there's nothing faster and cheaper than a lip-color upgrade. Marketing professionals call it "the lipstick effect" and it's a very real thing. You were probably feeling sad today and that's why you bought this book, am I right? And now you're filled with hope and joy. You're welcome, Denise.

Pencils, lipsticks, and glosses require very little skill and are very affordable and mix-and-match friendly. Have I worn a ninety-nine-cent gloss over a sixty-dollar lipstick? Absolutely. The same way I've hung my head out of a Tesla on the I-10 while eating peanut butter from a plastic spoon. It's called "high-brow, lowbrow" and it will always be in style. That brings us to our next section. . . .

BROWS

There is truly nothing more chic than clean skin, clean lashes, and an effortlessly sculpted brow. There's a queen I know (let's call her Ginger Minj since that's her name) who uses Sharpie on her eyebrows. Call me old-school, but I believe you shouldn't be able to personalize an eight-by-ten and arch your brow with the same tool. There are so many great brow products out there. (I happen to have a "sickening supply" of these products in my garage.) With the right product and technique, you can design a splash-proof brow that will get you through that third number at Hamburger Mary's Milwaukee and still leave you looking calmly surprised.

TOOLS

I saved this section for last because tools are the most important part of makeup. Makeup without quality brushes is like sex without quality lubricant. Either way, you end up looking like an irritated asshole.

In the lap of luxury, I enjoy MAC brushes. But Morphe and Sugarpill are some wonderful inexpensive options. And if you're a fan of me and Katya, you love nonfancy.

IN CONCLUSION

The most important thing to remember is that makeup is *optional*. If you pick your battles, you can get ready when you *feel like it*. Assemble a playlist, light a candle, and think of the process as a self-directed spa experience. I always put on the film *Clueless* or *Jawbreaker* when I need inspiration. But that's because I am a *woman*.

Let me caution you—painting your face different colors and textures won't make you un-hate yourself. I remember doing a blue smoky eye on a woman at the MAC counter. I buffed and blended for fifty minutes under department-store lighting—and even in that lighting, she looked CUTE-IFUL.* (Footnote: CUTE-IFUL: A mix between cute and beautiful. Stolen from my brilliant assistant Brandon Lim.) When I pridefully revealed the finished look, she took one look in the hand mirror and said, "I'm still fat." It was all at once that I understood that even a perfect makeup application can't change *everything.* You have to like yourself. You have to understand that a blue eyelid won't shave off fifty pounds. Brighter undereyes won't fix your dark childhood. But a good red lip will get you laid at your high school reunion and that is proof enough that makeup is God.

HEELS:

USING YOUR PLATFORM FOR GOOD!

by TRIXIE

WHAT TYPE OF HEELS ARE RIGHT FOR YOU?

Picture it: 2007. My roommate in the college dormitory has just been expelled for hitting his girlfriend, Claudia. I dim the lights ceremoniously and twist open an ice-cold Zima. I remove a forty-dollar patent-leather pump from a box and slip it on my squared foot (this was before I got my feet done). I queue up Marilyn Manson's version of "Tainted Love" and writhe on the freckled commercial carpet until my evening ballet class. My relationship with heels has just begun.

There is nothing more feminizing and empowering than heels. An easy essential in anyone's closet, a heel is a great way to heighten any look. Not just figuratively—they also make you tall. But what type is right for you? For me it's usually a chunky white go-go boot. For Katya it's usually a high-end deathtrap of a hooker shoe. Let's figure you out.

(PEEP TOES)　　　　　　　　　　　　(STILETTOS)

PEEP TOES

Let me ask you one simple question: Is your foot a slut? Does she come and go at all hours? Does she flash you that cigarette smile while she repaints her lips in Avon's Cherry Jubilee as if to say, "Everyone has a price"?

I'm mostly kidding, but peep toes are pumps with cleavage. But because they offer a flattering *peep* into your what's-gone-sour, peep toes do require the wearer to maintain an *excellent* pedicure. If you're a garbage person, skip the peep show and keep reading.

STILETTOS

If peep toes make your foot a slut, a stiletto makes your foot a fucking cock destroyer, babe. I've heard it said that women don't wear makeup for men; they wear it for other women. Same with stilettos. Stilettos communicate, "Yes, I *am* that slag you've seen in pornographic films. And if you so much as look at me wrong, I'll face-fuck your whole family."

Stilettos are the ultimate power move. The restriction of movement and mobility says, "I have nothing to do and nowhere to be. Now, go grab me a Sanpellegrino while I cross and uncross my legs for a Boomerang."

(CUTOUT HEELS)   (KITTEN HEELS)

CUTOUT HEELS

I was on the set of *RuPaul's Drag Race All Stars* season three. Ultimate hell hooker Morgan McMichaels endured hours of standing on the main stage wearing intricate, emerald, knee-high, cutout heels. RuPaul finally said, "Do you need a break? I remember in New York those strappy shoes would turn into razor blades after a few hours."

This story features what we in the professional poker industry call a "tell." If RuPaul can recall foot pain from his New York nightlife career, which was roughly forty-five years ago, cutout heels must truly *hurt*. The tradeoff is a very, very sexy foot moment. If self-injury is your gig, you can wear cutout heels to therapy.

KITTEN HEELS

One night, after a show, I noticed Latrice Royale step offstage and slip off her rotted little Lady Bunny heels. They were clear Lucite with a two-inch heel. I ribbed, "Latrice! Did these start off as *high* heels?" She said, "Try them on, bitch."

Ever the quintessence of fashion, I am open to new shoe experiences. I slid into the shoe—and I had my Oprah "Aha!" moment. These shoes won an instant honorary place in my closet. These shoes say, "I might not be tall or fashionable, but I am prediabetic."

(CONE HEELS)

(WEDGES)

CONE HEELS

Are you a casual witch who has a day job at an office that captions telephone calls for the deaf? Do you have textured skin? Do you say things like "It's not hot but it's humid"? Welcome to cone heels, so named for their ice-cream-cone shape. While the shape does give extra support, it's not worth inhabiting what is widely considered the fashion cone of shame.

PRO TIP:
You need one for each foot.

WEDGES

There was a girl named Nicole in my high school who had a death-defying tan and loved white wedges. She wore frosty-blue eye shadow to algebra and had an acrylic French-tip pedicure. She also listened to aggressive rap music, which is such a great look for a white teen in rural Wisconsin. I imagine today she is clocking in late for work at a vape shop in the mall.

Whatever happened to her, I thought her pedicure in a stacked wedge was the height of seduction. Wedges are maximum height, maximum comfort, maximum prostitute.

IN CONCLUSION

Platforms, oxfords, jelly sandals—there are many more options to explore. I would always encourage you to choose a style with the highest heel you can manage. People in the South say, "The higher the heels, the closer to God." Conversely, it can be concluded that the lower the heel, the closer to Satan. Amen.

PERSONAL STYLE:

WHO THE FUCK ARE YOU?!

a CONVERSATION with TRIXIE and KATYA

TRIXIE: I've been waiting for years for you to ask me about what it's like to have **personal** style.

KATYA: Nice. I'll start us off then! What's the difference to you between style and fashion?

T: I think style is your own internal compass regardless of what anyone else thinks or says is hot or is not. I think fashion is sort of more about the moment, the season, have you noticed that everyone's doing XYZ? Whereas personal style is more like: Oh yeah, that's what I like, that's why I do it.

K: Right. Or at least you know you have a radar. And it pings. Sometimes I feel like I might not be able to articulate exactly what I'm interested in at any given moment but I'll know it when I see it. That's for damn sure. And it's often at odds with whatever trend is hot and sizzling at the moment. Because who fucking cares about trends?

T: What is the difference between fashion and style to you?

K: I agree with you about style. And I think there's the world of fashion, or whatever, and then there's style, and then taste. And I think taste can be refined but it's not something that you can easily acquire. You kind of either have it or you don't in a way. It's almost like a musical gift. Of course you can practice and get really good, but sometimes you just don't have it.

T: I never thought of it that way. Wow, you mention people without musical gifts who keep persevering. I wonder why you're speaking to me . . .

K: (soft wheezy laughter)

T: Especially for drag, we sort of begin dressing up—like, when you are your gender, you start dressing that gender young, and you kind of figure it out over time. Then you're a twenty-year-old gay man who suddenly has to figure out women's clothing.

K: It's not always flattering; it's not always pretty; it's not always coherent. I'm fascinated by that beginning window of drag—the first few years where you know in your heart of hearts that you are that bitch.

T: For me, that never went away.

K: Well, right!

T: Sometimes when I think it's going to be a good look, but I haven't really tried it on yet, and then I put it on and it's not really what I envisioned. And it's all I have on me and I'm like, "I'm not really feeling it." You know? For dressing in drag at least, there's such a learning curve of learning your body, and what you have to do to your body to look like this imaginary body.

K: And also, what do you want to do with your body once you have that imaginary body onstage.

T: As drag queens, we're deciding everything: How old am I in drag? What am I like—am I fun-looking in drag? Or am I kind of like sexy and approachable?

K: Am I a total slut?

T: Yeah, am I the height of fashion? Or am I stuck in an era? Because drag queens are sometimes stuck in an era. Like Kasha Davis likes to live in an era a little bit. Or BenDeLaCreme, who lives in the sixties. Or like Detox, who gives a strong eighties vibe.

K: Futuristic eighties.

T: Which is Mugler, basically.

Yeah, totally. And then Violet's got a very defined retro-vintage wheelhouse I always like.

T: What do you do? What's your personal story line? When I look at old pictures of you as Katya, it was always—

K: Rotted.

T: Well, not rotted, but it was not always this sexualized Russian—

K: I went down three or four different avenues. I got sick of stuff really quickly. I'd do sexy gymnast whore, then I'd do campy, clown idiot. And then—

T: There's an incredible picture of you, I don't know if you remember it. You're wearing an Afro, with, like, headbands on?

K: Yeah. Crazy.

T: I can't believe that's even you. You have, like, clown lashes on! Do you own that picture? We should put that in the book.

K: I'm horrified looking at it. I'm also horrified of my old personal style. I transferred from Catholic school in third grade, made a big leap to public school in the fourth grade. I had to go back-to-school shopping! Up to that point, no clothes, just uniforms.

T: Okay, I have a question: Did you feel stifled?

K: Not at all. I felt relieved! I loved it.

T: Clothing has a hierarchy in elementary school. I would imagine if you all have the same uniform, it becomes about who has the best backpack?

K: Totally. Backpack, shoes, haircut.

T: Really? Wow.

K: Yeah! Or dick. Penis. Penis, dick, and balls.

T: Who has the most expensive penis, dick, and balls? Sure. Yeah.

K: So when I could choose my clothes, I would wear a silk blouse with a T-shirt underneath it in the same color. Both of those tucked in, but unbuttoned, into the same color shorts. So it was a monochromatic, casual, formal mess.

T: I'm covered, but I'm open. I'm transparent, but I'm layered.

K: It was so weird. One time I wore a polka-dot blouse, literally a silk blouse, with a bolo tie.

T: And look at you now. For me, over the years I developed the Trixie personal style. It was nice for me because of the Barbie thing. I didn't really know about fashion, but I had a model. If I did the same hair color and body type, I could see all the ways it's worked for someone else for five decades. I think it'd be a lot harder if you're doing drag and you have nothing to really emulate, at first.

K: Yeah. But out of drag, during the day, I do not care to stand out, because I get all that attention in drag.

T: We are literally both sitting here in black T-shirts. During the day, I am looking to be invisible.

K: I just like to maintain a very low profile, stick to the classics. And I don't get into trends. I like regular T-shirts, sweaters . . .

T: I do not get into trends. Especially in drag, I like the idea that if you open my closet everything kind of looks similar, like a cartoon person. I'm not looking to be like an ever-changing mannequin of hair colors and . . .

K: God, that's me. Well, not hair colors, but . . .

T: But, like, looks?

K: There's a lot of variation.

T: Yeah, I think it's a good thing to have a personal style that's streamlined enough that people could say, like, that's "very you." That's kind of a compliment because it means, like . . .

K: You've got a point of view. I was looking at Anna Wintour, personal style big-time: signature bob, unchanging since she was like *thirty,* and the same kind of very reliable, consistent aesthetic in terms of clothes and stuff. It's like a character.

T: I like when people blend the line between uniform, costume, and life clothes. Lisa Rinna, with her life uniform, that haircut.

K: Oh sure! And those lips.

T: RuPaul! In and out of drag. RuPaul said in one of her books, "Sometimes I change clothes three times a day." I don't know about that . . .

K: Yeah, that's kind of insane.

T: That is twenty-one looks a week.

K: That's a lot of dry cleaning. Oh, and what about Coco Peru! Totally identifiable silhouette.

T: See, I like that. The drag queens I always wanted to be like were like Bunny, or Coco Peru . . . it looks like they don't have more clothes.

K: I figured Coco had like sixty of those wigs just tucked away . . . she's got one.

T: It's just one. When she travels with it, she puts those little rollers in it at the bottom. She's actually very meticulous about it. Like every hair has to be in place. But again, she had a point of view. Coco Peru told me that when she first started doing drag, she thought of herself onstage, and she thought about the silhouette a spotlight would cast, and she was obsessed with the silhouette being a perfect flip hairdo, which is why her hair, no matter how she turns her head, it's the exact same shape.

K: Oh yeah, it's a bell.

T: Okay, let's say your house burned down—you're not in it, bummer—but let's say you have to replace your drag, and you have to make one phone call for a drag queen, like, "Hey, I need five looks for gigs." Who would you want? I would think Violet for you; she wears a lot of very nice black clothing.

K: Yes, but she shows her bare skin, and it's always way too hot and tight. Pain is an integral part of the fantasy, whereas I'm trying to avoid that.

T: I think I would say Lady Bunny because, comfort, you know.

K: Sharon Needles! I really love her style.

T: I like Sharon. I mean, for me, I like style that . . . maybe it's because I'm a fag, I like some kind of clear reference. I like to be able to look at someone and connect the dots. Not in an unoriginal way. But with Bunny, you're like, "Oh, it's Dusty Springfield meets . . ."

K: The Muffin Man.

T: Yeah. Or, I like when drag queens have the look that tells me what I'm gonna see.

K: Whose look do you think betrays their actual MO?

T: You.

K: Oh, okay, yeah.

T: Well, it depends on your looks. Because if you're in, like, one of your weird prairie dresses, I think something's coming down the pipeline.

Something's happening. But when you're, like, sexy in lace bodysuits, you would never think that the tongue's gonna come out and like . . . I'd never think you were gonna be *gross*! Not at the gay dancery! On the other end, I think with BenDeLaCreme's look, you know what you're gonna get.

K: It's certainly cohesive.

T: She has some of my favorite looks, because I think hers are pretty far in the opposite direction of fashion forward. Hers are almost costumes from a play. Whereas, I think where my makeup is crazy, I like my clothes and my hair to be somewhat inflated versions of real clothes.

K: Absolutely inflated. Inflated doll clothes.

T: Yeah! But even doll clothes are made based on normal clothes.

K: Yeah.

T: Regurgementation.

K: Regurgementation.

T: You know who I relate to and have always related to? There's this great scene in the film *Spice World*, where she goes, "I never know what to wear," and they go, "It must be really hard for you, Victoria, can't decide between the little Gucci dress, the little Gucci dress, and the little Gucci dress." I've always been like, that's the person I want to be.

K: But what do you think about aging stars and personal style? Like, for example, Madonna these days.

T: I think that she is so rich, and so iconic, that no one is stepping in. And I think someone should, because to let someone kind of go down in flames . . . but then again, look at somebody who's a Madonna stan? Fena Barbitall? Lives. She thinks Madonna is turning it.

K: Yeah, she lives, but she can appreciate her ironically, she gets the joke. She doesn't take her as seriously as Madonna takes herself. You know what I mean? Madonna has stans out there in their forties, fifties, and sixties that are, like, ride or die, will defend her every move no matter what? That's kind of crazy to me.

T: They're like, "You steal that baby, girl."

K: I saw her on *Graham Norton* the other day. She was wearing a bustier that was pushing her titties up to her chin, just this black lacey Sicilian-funeral kind of slut thing. And then just an eyepatch, a grill, and no sense of humor! She was humorless! It was shocking.

T: I want somebody to be like, "Let's dress up and take the piss out of it." I think Lady Gaga's looks, most of the time, have a post-fashion look. Like she's parodying celebrities. Especially in the beginning, she was parodying celebrity fashion culture.

K: Talk about changing three times a day?

TRIXIE: Do you remember when Lady Gaga went to the Met as both of us?

KATYA: She did three! She did me, you, and Julianne Moore. She really did!

TRIXIE: It was fierce! We can't get an invite, but . . . "

K: What would be your dream red-carpet style moment?

T: Like, who would dress me?

K: And where would you go?

T: Jeremy Scott. I would want to wear something from his past Moschino Barbie collection, or something from that *Wheel of Fortune* collection. Oh my God, that giant piece that was a TV dinner? It was a caftan but it was a TV dinner. And where would I be going? Kids' Choice Awards.

K: Oh yeah, slimed?

T: Yeah, jokey. Also, let me get close to the kids. I wanna know what they smell like. I just wanna know.

K: I think Jean Paul Gaultier would be great. Either him, Galliano, or maybe Viktor & Rolf or something—kind of out there, but still tethered to reality in some sense, but very theatrical.

T: I like when people have fashion that seems to have a jokiness to it. Because that's kind of what drag queens do. RuPaul said to me once, "You don't even know what you're doing. You're taking something in culture that already exists, and you're playing on it. You're parodying it, that's the whole Barbie thing. That's what Warhol does. And that's what a lot of fashion designers do." And I'd never even put that together. I think that's why I like Jeremy Scott so much, because he's like, "This thing everybody knows about? What if we made it a little stupider? And made it chic." I almost think he makes fun of fashion.

K: Are you kidding, he totally does! He trolls!

T: Do you have any fashion or personal-style pet peeves?

K: Yes, I do! Well, for drag queens, things I can't stand: number one, corsets as outerwear.

T: Oh my God! Raven? Raven puts corsets on as an outerwear and calls it a *corsette*.

K: Yeah, that is a trashy suburban thing. If you're wearing a corset as outerwear, your waist better be twelve inches. It has to be so severely cinched.

T: To me, there is no bigger sin than just a gown. Like, just a pretty dress. A pretty, sparkly dress that shows your body shape. To me, I'm just like, "Then what?" Honestly, even though I'm a drag queen, I've never been that into sequins. What do people hate on you for?

K: I've been accused of being too random, not trying hard enough, you know what I mean? Like, this is a thing I've heard a lot: "UGH, you could get away with anything."

T: I will say, you've set a precedent that your looks are intentional, and so you could make lazy choices and call it intentional.

K: Actually, I was really upset and unreasonably angry over something . . .

T: Expose her! Who was it?

K: Yvie Oddly. I saw some pictures of her from DragCon 2019 and thought to myself, Jesus Christ . . . this is a winner, right, she's like in her reigning year.

T: So she has money, and Katya doesn't, so she can shit talk.

K: It's not necessarily about having the money, it's the prestige factor, that you are crowned, and that's the queen of the castle, for a year. So, it's like, there's pressure—

T: It's not just pressure, it's also, you sort of, by winning, you have been verbally contracted that you'll bring honor to us all.

K: Represent the brand! Carry the torch for the year! But if you're firmly established with an aesthetic, all you've got to do is polish up a little bit, or present your best self. The bar is raised. But she went the other direction, and it seemed like . . . she was trolling. And on one level I don't care, because doing drag in itself is trolling. But on the other hand, you just look like a side of guacamole with lashes. You look like whodunnit and ran. You know what I mean?

T: When I get critical of newer queens, I always go . . . when did I become the queen I thought was the worst when I was twenty, who would try to give me tips, be critical of my drag, and I'd be like, "Fuck you, you're old." But I think I'm pretty accepting of all types of drag. I just want a maximum effort. I want you to paint me a detailed picture of something you're very clear on.

K: And that's the thing. It's funny how fashion, entertainment, and music can arouse such anger in a viewer—even something like drag, where the rules are meant to be broken. That's true, but also it's the effort, because it's the fantasy, the impact you can have selling the fantasy and making people gasp and inspiring people, or making people say, "Oh wow, that's really cool." And then you just show up in a T-shirt dress with some puffy paint on it? And some nasty makeup? Just stay at home! Stay at home and cultivate an air of mystique, you know what I mean? But anyway, I would feel so much pressure if I won the show, to constantly best myself. Look at somebody like Violet! Five years after, she is just getting better and better in terms of the looks.

T: Girl, there's a drag queen, and I don't wanna say who she is, because her name is Kim Chi, but one time we were chatting about looks and she said, "I know what people like about me, and I know what people don't think I'm good at." So she was like, "I know I can't do flips and stuff, so I take it very seriously to look incredible all the time." Willam! Whenever you tell Willam she looks pretty she will say, "Yeah, it's my job." Which I think is kinda rude, but . . .

K: Well, she's rude, but that's her thing. But, yeah, I appreciate that about Kim. It's all about having dignity and pride in what you do. I remember we were on the road with Fena and she would do my hair, but I couldn't imagine having somebody do my makeup. I have to do my own makeup because the sense of "I made myself look good" is so important to how I feel in drag that night and how I perform in that show. Do you know what I mean?

T: UH, absolutely. For me it's the entire sense of, like, pride. And I think drag queens get too preachy about, like, "I'm transforming . . ." Mary, you're the same person. But it does shift your gears to, like . . . you almost remind yourself, "I'm fucking fierce."

K: Yeah, "I'm that bitch."

T: Or, "I'm a bitch." Okay, now I'm wondering if people know, what's your go-to day look? Normal day, you're not flying, you might not see anybody.

K: Jeans, sneakers, T-shirt. But nice jeans, I'm wearing, like, really expensive jeans. No, actually, oh my God, I'm wearing Prada shoes today. They look like monster trucks.

T: Cool, do they match your monster face?

K: They're actually really cool. They're Frankenstein shoes.

TRIXIE: I think with personal style, it's always good to choose one thing people are going to remember about your look.

KATYA: The scabs.

TRIXIE: But, like, if you're going to wear a fun shoe, just wear a neutral everything else.

K: Yeah, absolutely. I don't get into flaunting conspicuous consumption or the label game. If those shoes are fierce, I don't care what they cost—I'm going to get them. Twenty dollars or a thousand dollars, it doesn't matter.

T: It's like cosmetics. I don't care about how much it costs, it's just gotta work. Or not work! Not working for me for twelve years. What's my go-to day look? Thank you so much for asking.

K: I know what it is!

T: I wear mostly black. And I like farmer shit.

K: I like you when you wear a sweatshirt. I like your sporty look.

T: My sporty look!

K: Yeah, your athleisure look is great.

T: Oh, thank you, yeah, I do a lot of a running pant with a sweatshirt. For a while I was really western. Okey Smokey. I was wearing cowboy hats. And then I got kind of bored of it, and now I just do more normal clothes. Because, honestly, when you're in drag so much we have to draw the line somewhere on, like, "I can't dress up when I'm out of drag." Anyway, what would you change about your personal style? If you didn't do drag, would you dress up more often?

K: No, I would just have more clothes, I think. And I would probably put more color into my wardrobe. I love staying classic because I want to keep clothes for a while! I always do black, gray, or red. Or just dark, dark colors, charcoal, whatever.

T: Do you wish you had hair?

K: No! Oh, on top? Absolutely I do!

T: Oh, I feel the opposite. I look back on when I had hair and I'm like, "You didn't know what to do with it when you had it." It does make people think you're young. Like, when I picture myself with hair, I'm like, "I think a lot more people wanted to fuck me."

K: With a thick, full hairline? Even if you shaved it?

T: I've had guys ask me, "On *Drag Race* you had hair, why'd you shave it, you were so hot with hair."

K: You looked like you were fourteen years old. You look like you've aged twenty-five years.

T: Yeah, I'm afraid to try to grow it back because I'm afraid—plot twist!

K: Is it gone?

T: Mama, Gone Girl. I mean, this is the hairline now. Well, getting realistic about your personal style is a great way to up your hotness. Having a shaved head? It can work or not work.

K: I have no choice. That's why I always wear a hat.

T: Do you remember having hair and wigs? Wigs want to slip off real hair. More than they want to slip off a shaved head.

K: Oh, this is like Velcro.

T: For drag, what's your favorite?

K: Favorite thing in drag? Well, if I could fucking control the AC? Then I just love something skin-fucking-tight. But I also love looking like a shiny, over-the-top, gaudy pattern problem, so much going on, just—the person you're going to look at in the room. First thing, "Who the fuck is that?"

T: I think you definitely bring that to the table. There could be a hundred people in the room . . .

K: It also depends on where you are, when in Rome. I do appreciate people who can acclimate and adjust to their surroundings. If I moved to Texas I might dress differently.

T: Every day as an adult, you're going to meet people you don't know, and your clothes can completely tell a story. I've got my western looks, I have my punk looks, I have headbands. Sometimes I go out and wear, like, leopard-print jeans and makeup if I want to feel real gay and dirty that day. And then I have my all-American-boy shit where I just wear like a white T-shirt and blue jeans. I try to tell a different story every time.

K: That's interesting, I don't really do that. I have a very tight wheelhouse. I don't get formal and I don't get– In LA, when it's very hot, I can get very casual. I boogie down Broadway. I don't like formal. I feel very– I worked at a bank for three years, bitch. I had to wear a suit and fucking tie.

T: That's all we've got! Takeaway is: if there's a little voice that says, "I think that would be cool"–listen to it. Unless you're Ginger Minj.

K: Yes! I watched an interview with Anna Wintour, and she said you have to have instincts, and you have to be able to trust that inner monologue, no matter what people are doing, it's risky.

T: No matter what anyone says, too. Truly, the people who pull off shit are the people who look like they wouldn't question it a day in their life. I've seen people who have an Anna Wintour haircut and a weird sunglass. If you present it, I believe it.

K: They sell it.

T: Alyssa Edwards says before you sell it you gotta buy it yourself.

PERSONAL HYGIENE:

WHOOPS, I'M DISGUSTING!

by KATYA

I'm a little embarrassed to admit that personal hygiene has always been an area of struggle in my life. Just recently, for example, I went three days without showering, due to sheer laziness and a brief but troubling fear of "hard water." Toward the end of day three, there was no measurable amount of Shalimar perfume capable of concealing my body's putrid aroma; my dandruff yield was Kilimanjaro-level heavy; and I could somehow smell the stench from my feet even while standing upright with my shoes on. My rotten body was desperate for a shower that night, but upon returning home, I was so exhausted that I shuffled right past the bathroom and into my bed fully clothed, with my shoes on. This is also known as a cry for help.

YOU CAN'T GET CLEAN OFF OF YESTERDAY'S SHOWER.

—WHISTLER'S MOTHER

Hygiene is not just important for our general health and well-being; it's also a vital public service that shows consideration for the people we come in contact with on a daily basis. When working in close quarters with others, such as in a well-populated office environment, it can be inconsiderate, alienating, and downright offensive to neglect one's hygienic state. It can also be detrimental to one's livelihood. Just ask recently terminated Sean Williamson, aka "Shit-smell-Sean," over there in Accounting—oh wait, you can't because he got fired for smelling like shit all the time.

But not to fear! You have options. I've always thought of fragrances (perfume, cologne, oil) as one of the most worthwhile splurges when it comes to shopping. With the right amount of a carefully selected fragrance, you become a welcome addition to any environment you set foot in. If it's day four with no shower and you show up for game night with the boys, then you are a tasteless affront to civilized culture and you risk the humiliation of getting hosed down in the garage by my uncle Frank.

Creating a morning hygienic ritual is a way to reset the body and mind as you scrub off the scum of yesterday's shame and prepare for whatever trials and humiliations the new day inevitably has in store for you. When you wake up in the morning, it is important to set the tone for the day. I like to jump out of bed, run to the bathroom, and stare in the mirror for a few minutes and give myself some positive words of encouragement like, "At least you still have your teeth! Now, get in the shower, you fucking bitch, and scrub the slime off that dead horse you call a body. Pronto!" (When you end a sentence with a foreign word, you invite a little culture into your life, and that's fun.)

I once dated a man who told me straight up to my face one day that I smelled like shit. I know, much like you must be at this moment, I was shocked, stunned, and blindsided by such an unexpected revelation. He had come over to my apartment that morning to engage in some romantic acts of a sexual nature, and having just woken up, I hadn't yet taken a shower, which

I didn't see as a problem because I wasn't a homeless wretch covered in feces. So I welcomed him into my bed, and as we tentatively approached third base (blow jobs), he recoiled and sat up to inform me in the politest way possible that I smelled like hot trash. He went on to explain that while he does enjoy a man's natural musk, mine was too pungent to stomach. Then he suggested I might benefit from a more robust brand of body wash than the usual organic unscented oatmeal bar that had faded to a sliver three months prior.

This was a lot to process for a person whose self-image holds no tether to an earthly reality. Sure, maybe it's true that I showered three days a week on average and only used soap on one of those days, didn't own shampoo, and considered myself "far too gay to smell that bad." But surely the real rotten truth stinking up the room was that his X-Men-level olfactory sense threatened my fragile self-esteem, and no amount of medical-grade mentholated body wash was going to change that. So I dumped him, or maybe we continued to date for a few more weeks until he dumped me, I don't remember.

What's clear to me now, however, is that this unprovoked personal attack was not a maliciously motivated attempt at character assassination but rather a sincere attempt at directly addressing an issue. If I had been in his place, I would have done what any other reasonably civilized person would do: dramatically avoided sexual contact for as long as possible and complained about his stench to every one of my friends until he found out about it.

Even armed with this self-awareness, it can be slightly hard to keep up the routine. If you are an outdoorsy type, you might find yourself on a very long camping trip without easy access to modern plumbing. Don't fret! I once worked with an insane woman named Linda who assured me that bathing in a stream or river is actually preferable to bathing in a shower or bath, and scrubbing the body with silt and sand is a natural exfoliant that leaves the skin refreshed and rejuvenated. It also increases the likelihood that you will be mauled by a bear, which is exciting.

THE WHORE'S BATH

As modern folk, we tend to take the simple things in life for granted. Just the other day, while I was helping my cool neighbor Karen power-wash the deer blood from the windshield of her beautiful brand-new Mazda Miata, I got to thinking, "Wow, where did we even get this hose, and where is all this water coming from?" Basic plumbing is an essential feature in the life of a modern woman, but sometimes, for reasons out of our control, a lady's gotta skip town without showering. That's when the power of perfume comes into play.

THE SMELL OF DEATH SURROUNDS YOU.

—LYNYRD SKYNYRD

Just like hookers would do in the olden days, all you need in lieu of an actual bath or shower is eighteen to twenty generous spritzes of a very strong and penetrating high-quality eau de parfum to mask the stench of your nasty ass.

WASH YOUR LEGS!

You wouldn't believe how many people do not bother to wash their legs while in the shower. History has proven that trickle-down economics didn't pan out for the working class, and the same applies here: Trickle-down soap and shampoo will not clean those gams, so do yourself a favor and give your soiled stems the due diligence they deserve.

PERSONAL HYGIENE: WHOOPS, I'M DISGUSTING!

YOU CAN LEAD A HORSE TO WATER, BUT YOU CAN'T MAKE IT BRUSH ITS TEETH.

—ENRIQUE IGLESIAS

AN INCONVENIENT TOOTH

If the eyes are the windows to the soul, then the mouth is the grand foyer of the head, complete with a red-carpet tongue and ivory-staircase teeth. Sounds glamorous, right? But you don't need to be rich to have a million-dollar smile. That's right, with just a few hundred thousand dollars and a year of hiding from the public at home in surgical convalescence, you, too, can have a Julia Roberts–level megawatt Hollywood smile.

Let's be honest: Going to the dentist is about as fun as driving over a beloved pet on the way home from dialysis. From my earliest memories until the present day, every dentist's office that I have gone to has taken a ghoulishly violent approach to my dental health, as if my mouth contained a great evil that can be banished only through a cartoonish level of pain. One time I had to look up and make sure that it was a dental tool and not a diesel-fueled chainsaw that she was using to hack into the sensitive tissue of my gum line. But it is a necessary evil, so we soldier on twice a year and pay too much in dental insurance to ensure our smile is our best accessory, not a gaping maw of festering brown Chiclets staggered atop grayish mounds of putrid necrotic tissue.

1. Get a tongue scraper and scrape your tongue first thing after you wake up in the morning. They are so cheap! So simple and yet so darn effective. The first time I scraped my tongue, I wondered aloud who could have snuck into my bedroom to dump the slimy contents of their compost bin into my mouth. I don't know if I'll ever come to terms with the harsh reality that my body is less a wonder and more a wasteland, but now I have a fun new way to see it for myself.

2. Brush, floss, and rinse at least twice a day, NO EXCEPTIONS. Invest in a high-quality electric toothbrush, stock up on floss, and keep a nice giant bottle of antiseptic mouthwash in the cupboard. If you're a low-bottom alcoholic, or living in a halfway house, you can avoid temptation by choosing the alcohol-free substitute, which works just as well. It's a lovely grounding ritual and you will be grateful later on, when your teeth are still inside your mouth and not hanging below it from a necklace you've made at Thursday's voodoo craft night.

3. Buy a Waterpik. This is a device that shoots a tiny but powerful stream of liquid. It's basically a quick floss and rinse in one. I love it. You can also spray disobedient pets with it, or fill it with liquor for some controlled and precise drinking.

4. Research your dentist, feel them out, shop around. If you can't afford dental insurance, I feel you—times are tough, and in this economy, I'd recommend you steal everything you need from CVS, which brings me to my favorite pastime and claim to fame:

5. BLEACH THOSE BROWN CHICLETS! The only time in my life when I adequately planned ahead for an important event was when I bleached my teeth before I appeared on television. I've had these teeth for nearly four decades, and I've treated them to a steady intake of tobacco, coffee, and corrosive chemical poisons, so before the bleach, these pearly whites were more shades of autumn. You don't need them too blinding white unless the creepy game-show-host look is what you're after. It took me only about three packs of professional-strength Crest Whitestrips used over a six-month period to go from jaundiced burlap to a crisp, bright ivory. Just be sure to set a timer for the strips, because if you leave them on for longer than thirty minutes (or, God forbid, fall asleep with them on), it will feel like your enamel is dissolving into your face in just a few hours and it's the worst feeling in the world.

6. If your dental situation is truly off the chain and there's no hope in sight, you can just wear a knockoff designer-print surgical mask all day! It'll curb your embarrassment and mask that gnarly breath while providing a welcome layer of mystique to your look.

STOP! HAMMERTOE

In the movie *Boomerang,* notorious playboy Marcus is in bed with yet another beautiful one-night stand, and as he pulls up the covers on the sleeping woman's otherwise perfect body, he is shocked by the ghastly, unkempt state of her toes. The following day, he relays his disappointment about her feet to his friends by declaring, "It was hammer time." That phrase has stuck with me since the nineties, and it is one that continues to both haunt and motivate me to maintain at least a rudimentary level of care toward my constantly abused lower limbs.

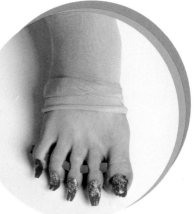

I really don't like getting pedicures. I've gotten maybe a half dozen in my life, and each time I wonder why I subject myself to the same strange series of uncomfortable sensations in a scenario that makes me inherently uneasy. The soles of my feet are so ticklish in spots that my legs lurch and nearly kick the nail tech in the face. Then I stare in horror as she uses gardening shears to clip my toenails, obsessing about how easy it would be to absentmindedly snip off my entire big toe. Then I get self-conscious about being too faggy as the only guy in the salon, and then I become paranoid about being a bougie white stereotype, and before you know it, it's time to dry my feet off and they didn't even do the only enjoyable part: using an industrial kitchen tool to scrape off thick chunks of dead foot skin.

Nevertheless, it is important to acknowledge the overburdened nature of our feet and to reward their hard work from time to time. If you're not the pampering type like me, and would rather chew on a tinfoil sandwich than get a pedicure, even a ten-minute soak in a bowl of warm water with Epsom salts once a week can make all the difference.

ALOCHOL

(SORRY, I'VE BEEN DRINKING)

by TRIXIE

A GUIDE TO LIQUOR

There's an old adage some people swear by: You booze, you lose. Well, if that's the truth, explain the crown in my living room next to the wastebasket full of empty cans of wine.

I'll never forget my first taste of "the sauce." I was maybe six years old, sitting on my grandpa's lap at the kitchen table. He poured himself shot after shot of blackberry brandy until I finally said, "I want some!" To my immense surprise, he encouraged me to take a sip.

Most people who enjoy drinking have fond memories of their first drink. Not me. This blackberry brandy touched my six-year-old tongue with all the fury of Kim Davis in 2015. As my last remaining taste buds disintegrated, I felt betrayed. Why would anyone ever enjoy this?

Then I went to college. I was dating a hipster at the time, so the rattails and ironic band tees hit me like a hurricane. I'd be at house parties all the time where the artsy kids would drink seemingly competitively. After weeks of standing in parties pretending to enjoy the free drink, I actually started to understand how people enjoy the taste of booze: They DON'T. They endure the taste to get drunk.

But which type of liquor is for you? That depends on a lot of factors: what you're wearing, what you want to feel like, whether or not you're trying to convince your date that you're "masc." Skip the date—let me take you on a speed date of all your eligible singles! (Or doubles if you can hold your booze!)

WHISKEY

Whiskey is made from fermented grain mash and is aged in charred wooden barrels. Not sounding sexy? That's because whiskey is not sexy. It's trashy. At my chubbiest and most depressed, I used to drink Jack and ginger. I'd perch at the bar at Flaming Saddles all alone on a Monday and request Dixie Chicks songs until I could no longer fully pronounce "Sin Wagon."

I think straight guys drink whiskey because they think that enduring a putrid brown liquid makes them seem tough. Women drink it because they want to feel like they are Carrie Underwood or some faux-western version of a cartoon cowgirl. Gays drink it because their abusive fathers drank it and it makes them feel close to their dads but not in arm's reach.

Since darker liquors are more complex, they are more difficult for the body to break down. They feel more mushy and warm and emotional than other boozes and have less of an "upper" feeling. If you cry during the animated film *Up*, stay away from this drink. You'll be desperately trying to text your ex but not able to accurately use the T9 on your cracked Motorola Razr.

Booze is booze. Whiskey is still a wondrous thing. When I was on whiskey, I remember feeling cool when I ordered it. But after six months, I decided that hot cinnamon diarrhea wasn't really *my thing*.

BOURBON

If whiskey is the country-bumpkin black-footed hollerbaby of booze, bourbon is its rich cousin who goes to the Kentucky Derby and wears suits in eighty-five-degree heat. Bourbon is whiskey made in the United States, typically in Kentucky. (Did you know 96 percent of the world's reserves of bourbon come from Kentucky?!) They actually age bourbon in barrels that were formerly whiskey barrels. This partially explains the more complex taste (of fruit, floral, and nut—in my butt? what?) of America's Native Spirit.

What qualifies as bourbon? A real-life noncatfished bourbon has to be aged in a barrel for at least two years. The mash must also be at least 50 percent corn. So if you do the math on two years and 50 percent corn, it makes sense that it also gives you 150 percent qualified violent diarrhea.

I dated a guy in Kentucky (see the chapter titled "Breakups") and he introduced me to bourbon. At first it made me feel cool and southern and rich, but eventually after breaking up I realized I only drank it to impress him. (It didn't work, by the way.)

VODKA

Vodka is like Katya: Russian, low-calorie, and made from old potatoes. Vodka is probably in the cheapest, grossest concoction at a college party—and *also* in the fanciest highball at the hotel bar. Vodka is supereasy to make taste good and absolutely makes you drunk. Gays love it—I've even heard vodka soda referred to as "gay water."

Vodka is also pretty good across all price points. You can impress your Tinder date with Grey Goose, or mix Fleischmann's with purple Gatorade on Milwaukee public transit in 2009 and throw up on your boyfriend in front of his friends from out of town. Nowadays I like SKYY vodka. It's affordable and smooth. Plus they put me on billboards (even though the billboards catch fire sometimes OMG google my Times Square billboard on fire).

Vodka comes in a million different colors and flavors, which also makes it fun. If you serve someone a fancy-tasting drink, they'll think you're fancy and they'll tell their friends. Word spreads and next thing you know, you'll be having pink vodka lemonades with Anderson Cooper on a boat. I once went to BenDeLaCreme's house and he served me a fancy drink, and, bitch, my wig FLEW. He started out as a very gracious host but then he suddenly left . . . which is so unlike him!

You might be thinking, but, Tracy . . . how do I make a pitcher of vodka lemonade for my friends? I can teach you! I once was nominated for a James Beard Foundation Award for making a cocktail at *GQ*.

2 cups ice

180 ml SKYY vodka

80 ml lime juice

80 ml cranberry juice

60 ml Malibu

1.25 qt lemonade
(fresh with no pulp is best)

I always finish it with a sprinkle of edible glitter and a bright paper straw. With cross-dressing and drinking, presentation is everything! I'm **TELLING YOU:** People will think it's so cool and it really makes something like a normal friend coming over on a normal day feel really gay.

TEQUILA

Let's just stop everything right now and call tequila what it is: *dark-sided*. Tequila's active ingredient is ethanol, which is a central nervous system depressant. This means your self-control is depressed. Tequila is that booze that makes people fight, dance, and ultimately puke, like a Dr. Pimple Popper video set to a Shakira song.

That being said, tequila has a very "up" feeling compared to other alcohols. After a long workday, let's say you want to meet your friends for a happy-hour moment. A shot of tequila will help you start off your evening without immediately getting tired from that first drink. You could also try narcotics. (See: Katya.)

GIN

Gin is completely misunderstood. Gin and tonic is usually my drink of choice; I love it. It's light, bright, and difficult to mess up.

I can already hear you saying, "It tastes like pine needles!" It really doesn't. Gin is distilled with juniper berries and flowers. When you imagine those flavors as you take a sip, the sweetness pops out, I promise. It makes me think of wearing a floral crown while watching my unfaithful lover burn to death in the corpse of a dead bear.

It's hard to imagine that gin was ever meant to be enjoyed neat because it's SO intense. But, OMG, mixed with some fruit-flavored sparkling water from 7-Eleven and finished with a cute little flower blossom? Bitch, it is OVER for vodka soda. Vodka soda found bald and decomposing. (See: Katya.)

BOTTOM- S'UP?

Keeping your drinking habits classy has a lot to do with whether or not you can enjoy it long-term. You want people at parties to be whispering, "Who's that girl?" for the *right* reasons. When I was nineteen, I saw my drunk roommate shit herself into her tights in a miniskirt. As a not-hard-enough turd snaked down her sheer Urban Outfitters tights, I knew I'd never unsee it. Whenever you see someone too messy, remind yourself that you're always only a few sips from shitting your tights.

PILLS, PIPES, AND POTIONS:

OVER THE RAINBOW AND UNDER THE INFLUENCE

AN EDUCATION IN DRUGS

by KATYA

If you've ever wondered what it would be like to dance naked in the middle of a dirt road at three a.m. as the night sky melts into the pulsating fleshy oven mitts that used to be your hands, then I've got something that will do the trick. Drugs! Sure, they're scary, they're dangerous, and they're mostly illegal, but they're also a lot of fun, and I've done most of them and I'm still here—alive and healthy enough to string together just enough intelligible sentences to rule out any significant long-term brain damage.

Now, I know that you are still a developing young woman—and by the way, you are looking great, and I am so proud of you—so it would be downright reckless and irresponsible of me to encourage anyone in such a sensitive condition to chemically alter their body and mind with narcotics. I knew a girl named Hannah who took an entire bag of magic mushrooms in the sixth grade. While the details of what happened next are too disturbing to share, let's just say that when she emerged from the hospital a week later, she would only answer to the name "Lieutenant Zardon," and when pressed for details about what happened, she would lean down and whisper, "General Grant will return for The Leg." We never did find out what happened to The Leg, but it serves as an important cautionary tale: When it comes to drugs and other risky recreational activities like free-climbing, sometimes the juice ain't worth the squeeze.

But who am I to talk? Some of my fondest memories of growing up in the bland Caucasian suburbs feature drugs in some way. As teenagers, we had limited access to most illegal fare, so often we made do with inexpensive over-the-counter items. One day, a group of us skipped school and went to CVS to shoplift bottles of Robitussin cough syrup. "Robo-tripping" turned out to be a roller-coaster event, as we downed a bottle each and then immediately proceeded to barf our brains out. Then we experienced a nauseating few hours of a high that for me produced a strange bright red skin rash that migrated (or at least it appeared to) from the crown of my head all the way down to my feet over the course of the trip. For those not keen on nausea, sucking the gas out of a whipped-cream canister offers a quick loopy buzz that's pretty fun, although I always got the distinct impression that I could actually feel my brain shedding thousands and thousands of its precious neurons with each puff.

At the same time, we had to suffer through those awkward "scared straight" presentations at school, where former addicts come to warn us about the dangers of using drugs by sharing darkly vivid and inappropriate stories from their using life. I'll never forget the strange man who had suffered so much damage from snorting vast amounts of cocaine, he would blow snot rockets of decaying nasal tissue in the shower each morning and would have to push them down the drain with his big toe. So that's fun. Still, nothing says party time like a little bit of cocaine. I can think of no other drug more glamorized than this one, and its popularity has remained relatively steady throughout the decades. And, really, can you think of a more chic and glamorous activity than awkwardly snorting high-priced, low-grade nose candy off a douchebag hedge fund manager's flaccid weenie? Party!

Another popular option: Have you done a weed? We'll keep this section brief, as marijuana has blown up recently, and as it enters the legal marketplace you can just go ahead and do your own damn research on it. I have smoked a lot of weed in my life, so I will share this: A while ago, my therapist, who specializes in substance abuse, told me that marijuana, especially the potent strains available today, can cause psychosis. I told that woman to get the heck out of town, grabbed my purse, and stormed out of the office (to use the bathroom), and when I came back inside, I told her about some disturbing events that had taken place in my head space. The common denominator throughout was guess what! That's right—the reefer. So, if you are prone to paranoia, magical thinking, flights of fancy that steer you away from important activities like showering, eating, or tending to wounds, then you might want to reconsider puffing on the good-good, as it may not be ideal for your psychological setup.

If that kind of thing sounds fun, though, there are even more options. "I'm just, like, a very visual person," says Marie, who prefers to understand and process her surroundings through the act of looking around rather than, say, touching or licking them. Most people without a visual impairment are quite visual, and one of the coolest things we can do as visual creatures is severely alter the way we see the world by taking psychedelic drugs that cause major mind-blowing hallucinations. I did a lot of LSD and mushrooms while I languished in the suburbs, and I gotta tell you, a good trip can really spruce up a dull neighborhood. I once watched an hour-long Radio City Music Hall Rockettes Christmas Spectacular show take place inside the carpet of my bedroom. Man, can those girls kick! There is, of course, the looming danger of the cursed "bad trip," which is always a possibility. (See: Hannah and The Leg.) I saw for myself once when I took two hits of LSD, dyed my hair bright orange, and got stuck staring at my reflection in the bathroom mirror for about two hours, locked in a very unpleasant existential quagmire about the nature of my physical identity.

Sometimes a dreary life needs a little bit of a pick-me-up, but rather than seeking a healthful, organic approach like ginseng and turmeric, we turn to drugs. Why? 'Cause they're fast and they work. Let's take a look at a few of the more high-powered engine revvers and consider the pros and cons of life in the fast lane.

Amphetamines are available in a prescription in different forms—many of them formulated specifically to prevent recreational abuse—and are used to treat attention deficit hyperactivity disorder. For the average person, however, amphetamines, or speed, do exactly what the name suggests: They get you behind the wheel of a bus with a bomb strapped to it and hopefully, with the help of a handsome Hollywood leading actor, you'll manage to get yourself

and all those passengers to safety. Just kidding—there is no amount of pep pills that will transform you into Sandra Bullock. Believe me, I've tried.

If you decide to abuse prescription drugs, one upside is that you get to know exactly what and how much you are consuming. When you buy illegal drugs off the street, you really don't know what the actual contents of those drugs are. I once tried to buy cocaine from a man named "Sheet-Rock" and I ended up with a hundred-dollar bag of wood chips. My nose was sore for three weeks. That being said, with frequent use, prescription drugs incur the same amount of damage—and sometimes the dependency can be more intense on account of their purity.

Whether they're prescription pills or not, when it comes to uppers I like to think of the old adage "If you dance with the devil, don't be surprised to find a pitchfork up your ass," or something like that. Or to put it more simply, "What goes up must come down," and this basic truth will never be more apparent than it is to the sleep-deprived crank-head running on fumes as they finally crash-land into bed after a bender. The comedown from even a weekend speed binge can be brutal, and if you've been sautéing your central nervous system on the regular for weeks, months, or God forbid longer—then you can most likely expect the crash to feel meteoric in scale, and it's going to take a lot of time to crawl out of the crater.

Downers are a whole other game. All these years, I thought it was just a figure of speech when my neighbor Greg would say, "Hey, man, just take a chill pill." As I look back at my childhood more carefully, I realize what Greg was actually doing, which was trying to get me to take a prescription benzodiazepine with a glass of water, usually while I was having a seizure. Chill pills come in all forms, many of them legal and widely distributed to the anxious throng of overmedicated America. In my wildly incomplete and unprofessional assessment of the collective American psychological profile, I would say that people have become far too dependent on chemical relief when it comes to anxiety.

You young folks might hear an "Old" like me declare: I remember when being scared was just a regular part of life! Large crowds, paranoia, public speaking? Stuttering through a book report while pissing your dungarees was practically a rite of passage in my middle school, and a tradition that I carried proudly into college.

Thankfully, heroin is one of the few drugs I've never done, and to this day I still don't really understand its appeal. It has never seemed chic, glamorous, cool, or interesting. From what I can glean from the movies and real-life anecdotal evidence, it's a really fun way to fall asleep standing up in the middle of the street, and an excellent way to choke to death on your own vomit when you're tuckered out in bed after an exhilarating bout of diarrhea. I'll just take the word of a longtime junkie friend I knew in Boston who after decades of being down-and-out finally kicked her habit. "It feels like you are wrapped in the warmest, most comfortable blanket of pure bliss, joy, and love and complete satisfaction," she said. "And then you get to spend the rest of your life trying to get back to this rush, while it fades away and grows more elusive with every try, as your life quickly disintegrates all around you." Fuck.

I'm not a huge fan of telling people what to do (which is why I've decided to write an advice book), but when it comes to drugs, dear reader, I'll just sum it up by telling you what I would tell my own daughter: Don't bother—they're really not worth it. You could emerge unscathed, you could develop a nasty habit, or you could spiral into addiction and then be saddled with the daily trudge of recovery (like me!) for the rest of your life. But one thing's for certain—doing drugs won't make you cool and won't make you happy. You've already figured out how to be happy (you bought this book). All you need to do now is buy ten more copies and you'll be cool.

SELF-LOVE:

by KATYA

AUTOEROTIC APPRECIATION

A GUIDE TO SELF-CARE

You know what I love? Me. That's right, dear reader, I am not ashamed to tell you that I am absolutely head over heels in love with myself, and I love to sanctify this love with wonderful acts of nourishing, rejuvenating, and replenishing self-care all throughout the week.

If we are talking about developing and nurturing a relationship with oneself, I prefer an expansive and multifaceted approach. Setting aside any physical activities and rituals we do in the interest of self-care, let's first focus on the emotional, psychological, and metaphysical implications of what it actually means to love oneself. Do you love yourself? Do you? What does this even mean? Who is the you and what is the self?

I find it's best to avoid chasing these often tempting existential quandaries down a dead-end rabbit hole, as they inevitably lead to doubt, confusion, and sadness. Instead, you can perform simple, straightforward gestures of self-love like stopping at the mirror on the way out of the house and giving your reflection a bright and hearty thumbs-up.

You can up the ante on special occasions when reinforcements might come in handy. If I'm leaving the house to go on a first date, I'll fortify my self-esteem with pickup-line affirmations from my favorite romantic comedies. "You had me at hello," I'll earnestly whisper at the mirror and then inevitably blush and wave back. Then I'll linger in the mirror a little longer and coyly address my reflection thusly: "Roses are red, violets are twisted, bend over, sweetheart, you're about to get fisted!" That never fails to perk up the self-esteem.

Ask anyone and they will tell you, successful long-term relationships often require a lot of work and involve a fair amount of compromise, and it's no different with the individual's relationship with the self. I mean, you can't get much more long-term than that, unless you dissociate, are lobotomized, or fall into an irreversible coma, in which case: hurray for you. So just like in any marriage, friendship, or prolonged hostage situation, our relationship with numero uno will be fraught with moments where we are dissatisfied, annoyed, repulsed, or just plain hate the fucking guts of our dear life partner, aka ourselves.

In such inevitable periods of floundering self-worth, I find it helpful to imagine that I have a severely developmentally disabled, quadriplegic, radiation-poisoned dog named Tabitha. I certainly wouldn't berate her for hours and hours about all the goals she has yet to accomplish, nor would I ever viciously mock her mangy fur or mercilessly bully her about her lack of ambition, her laziness, or her poor decision-making skills and chronic tardiness. After all, she can't even read a clock (she's also blind). Then I try to summon the same level of compassion I would naturally feel toward Tabitha and apply it to myself, and the result is often remarkable. I pat myself on the head and in a very loud, slow, and patronizing tone, say out loud, "You're doing the best you can, sweetie. Or maybe you're not, but it's fine, don't worry. Everything's going to be okay." The more helpless and disadvantaged you can envision yourself, the greater the amount of compassion you'll be able to embody, and the better equipped to wade out of these stormy pockets of self-doubt without psychologically torturing yourself to death.

Self-love is all about action, and I'm not talking about masturbation, you fucking pervert. (I'll get to that in a moment.) It's hard to love yourself if you don't do anything nice, meaningful, helpful, creative, responsible, or productive. There's a great saying: Self-esteem comes from doing esteemable acts. This is all relative, of course, and it's not to say that doing good things will make you happy. Look at Mother Teresa—she was a complete bitch! (But what a legacy.) Anyway, the next time the relationship with yourself has hit a rough patch, a simple glance at your daily activity log might hold some clues as to why you hate yourself.

Have you called out of work three days in a row this week and spent the majority of your day motionless on the sofa watching QVC while shoveling dozens of 7-Eleven–brand frosted mini-doughnuts into your face? Wow! I would hate myself too, so it's time to get off the couch and go do something of value, perhaps an activity that seems fun but a little scary, like teaching volleyball down at the local orphanage, learning how to read, or finally talking to someone about that dislocated shoulder.

QUIZ: From Self-Loathing to Self-Loving

Answer these questions either TRUE or FALSE to determine the amount (or lack) of passion you've got for yours truly.

1. I fantasize about my death. A lot.

2. I have a hard time deciding what to eat for lunch because the voices tell me I'm not worthy of nourishment.

3. I didn't ask to be the most beautiful person alive; it just happened.

4. Most days I want what's best for myself, but society won't let me wiggle.

5. I tend to avoid mirrors because I am way too aroused by my own reflection.

6. I actually love mirrors because every time I check my reflection, someone different is looking back.

7. I believe everything will work out in the end, as long as my legs don't get too wet.

8. I draw strength from the fact that God has chosen me alone to help thwart the devil's master plan for Armageddon.

9. Sleeping is a luxury that my wicked body does not deserve.

10. I'm me, and I'm here, and I want that.

Once we've answered the all-important question of "Do you love yourself?" in the affirmative, then congratulations! It's time to take a break. So sit back, sit down, relax, and find a seat, while we dive into the more practical world of self-care.

For the modern woman, it can be quite difficult to make the time to relax, unwind, and unplug, especially in today's ultra-fast-paced, achievement-oriented, workaholic-prone culture. In some circles, if you aren't working eighty hours a week in addition to maintaining a half dozen semiprofessional-level hobbies while dating two or three potential life partners in between your volunteer shifts at the aquarium, then you are basically a good-for-nothing lazy piece of shit. For the all-too-common overachiever, the concept of taking a break is not just simply out of the question; it's categorically impossible. "I'll sleep when I'm dead" is their motto, and as far as I'm concerned, death can't come soon enough for these miserable wretches, who would surely benefit from being physically restrained and wheeled out Hannibal-Lecter style to the beach or the forest for a few hours every week.

OPTION 1: I'M THE ONE THAT I WANT

One of the best things to do when we have to make a tough decision is to sleep on it. But an even better thing we can do is jerk off on it. For example, say it's Friday night and you are all alone, languishing in front of the television, numbly watching exercise equipment infomercials in Spanish, when it occurs to you that now would be a great time to text the ex-boyfriend and see if he might want to come over and do sex to you. Were this ex not an untrustworthy sociopath and overall complete piece of shit, there wouldn't be much of a problem here. But if we let our libido build up, we run the risk of becoming overrun with desire, so much so that our standards fly out the window with our lace panties. Follow that path and before you know it, that shitty ex is back in the picture—or, perhaps more likely, you're boning that shifty

vagrant who was eating out of the trash earlier and now he's sound asleep (and quietly urinating) in your bed.

Next time you feel lonely and are about to engage in some questionable behavior that will undoubtedly carry some very unwelcome consequences, take a deep breath, find a quiet space, and jerk off! In a matter of seconds, the post-orgasm brain will be clearer and unencumbered by carnal distractions so we can make rational, logical decisions less likely to put our well-being at risk.

Make sure you have all the props and toys and tools that you need to arrive at the peak of Mount Orgasm, and when shopping for sex toys and treats, don't be afraid to splurge! Just as cheap toilet paper is NOT a bargain, the same goes for erotic accoutrements. If something is going in your ass, mouth, or pussy, then it better be top shelf, and in the spirit of self-care, that's a rule you should really apply across the board.

OPTION 2: YOU'RE DOING AMAZING, SWEETIE

If you've ever been on an airplane, then you'll probably recall the flight attendant telling you that in the event of an emergency, if the oxygen masks drop down, you should secure your own mask before you attempt to help those around you. This instruction can apply to our lives as well, in a broader sense. As a gay person, I am prone to hyperbole and high drama and will catastrophize even the slightest inconvenience to the level of global crisis. I am usually fifteen seconds away from spiraling toward suicide, as the cabin pressure of my life is permanently set to "Well,

it's over." It's something I'm working on, but I've learned that if I consistently apply my mask by tending to my effective self-care routines, then I will not only be available to participate in and enjoy my life, but also be a radiant beacon of joy for those around me. They say God helps those who help themselves, which is just a religious justification for selfishness, but I'll take it.

DAILY AFFIRMATIONS

Look in the mirror and repeat the following twice a day or more, as needed:

"I am a good person and I deserve to be happy."

"I have a bright future ahead with many wonderful possibilities in store for me."

"I am definitely not a criminal and I do not enjoy breaking the law."

"I wonder what it sounds like when a teenager is buried alive."

"I have many talents and I love to share them with the world."

"Burying pots and pans in the backyard is not a worthwhile activity."

"When I smile, I let the world know that life is good and I am happy."

"There's nothing wrong with my legs and it's okay that they're always wet."

MORE OPTIONS:
ADDITIONAL SELF-CARE STRATEGIES

The Basics:

- Sleep eight hours a night

- Eat three meals a day

- Drink ten tall glasses of water a day

- Connect with nature

- Listen to a joyful song

- Smile at a child (no touching)

- Feed the ducks by the lake

- Send a handwritten letter to Grandmom

- Chase a turkey into a slaughterhouse

- Lend a helping hand to a person who has fallen down

- Establish firm but respectful boundaries with coworkers

- Consume an entire Thanksgiving Day meal in your car

Take a moment each day to convince yourself that everything's fine and it could very well get even better, but it's only likely to happen if you can keep your legs dry.

PART TWO

AKING

MONEY :

ARE YOU A POOR?

FINANCIAL ADVICE BY TRIXIE AND KATYA

TRIXIE:

T he legendary band ABBA says "Money, money, money! Must be funny in the rich man's world!" Let me tell you that that assumption is factual and sound. Since becoming a television and folk music star, I have been witness to many bizarre indulgences of the upper echelon. Bidets, central air-conditioning, luxury cosmetics. I personally know people with enough face and body work done to finance a small business during that grappling first year.

While money can definitely bring you custom sofas, brow lifts, and fat transfers performed in Mexico, I have found such indulgences also prove indicative of deeper cracks in our veneered surfaces. We are obtaining and collecting to balance out our perceived personal shortcomings. And it doesn't stop there. No person has had one nose job—he's had three. By the third procedure he has probably live-streamed the process in exchange for a free eyebrow threading. I once took a photo with someone I didn't know for a free pair of sunglasses I didn't want—only to get home, try them on, hate them, and then wish I had asked for two pairs.

The danger in finding financial comfort is the inevitable adjustment to your new means. Suddenly, the lifestyle of yesterday will seem dim and institutional. The first Delta One flight will make Economy Comfort Plus seem like a sexual punishment. Suddenly, last year's iPhone is basically a beeper. And an UberPool seems like a bizarro *ElimiDate* episode you never asked to be a part of.

Whether you are rich or poor, it's important with money to keep yourself balanced. Upon becoming a "richie," I checked in on some of my favorite ways to live cheap:

1. Bitch, I love biking. The speed, the danger, the wind in my nonexistent hair! My bike cost me two hundred fifty dollars—think about it. An Uber in LA is at least ten bucks (See the chapter titled "Travel"), so twenty-five bike rides later I got me a FREE BIKE. People are always confused when they see me walk in with a helmet in tow. "Did you bike here?" *No, bitch, I took a Lyft but I'm just cautious and prone to seizures. DUH.* I am always asked then, "Do you need a ride?" *No, bitch, I have my bike, WHICH IS A RIDE.*

And, girl—invest in a bike lock. And lock it *around* the front tire. I recently had my front tire stolen at a Target while I was inside picking up a few Barbies. I exited the store to find an elderly male security guard informing me that a "black tranny and her dyke friend" stole my tire. He then showed me footage of a displaced trans woman yoinking

my precious front wheel. I decided not to press charges. Firstly, she probably needed it more than I do. Secondly, could you imagine the news headline? *"Drag Race* Star Trixie Mattel Prosecutes Homeless Trans Woman of Color." Yikes! I hope the woman is enjoying my bike tire at least. A brisk bike ride can be a fabulous alternative to a salon blowout.

2. Steal Netflix and Hulu. This might sound a little tacky, but let me be honest with you. My ex-boyfriend's mother died of lung cancer and I found out because the Netflix I had been stealing for three years expired. I was devastated—but I was desperate to find out whether or not they were going to Make Him a Murderer or not. I promptly created an account, and while I enjoy not having my "continue watching" section flooded by Tammy's reality programs, I do fondly recall my three years of savings.

3. Find a richer and more stylish friend your size. I have two or three comrades who are exactly my height and proportionate to me in every way. However, there is one difference: Their closets are lined with fox fur and gold, and mine is filled with drag-queen T-shirts and gym shorts I stole from my ex in 2010. When I have to appear somewhere and look truly chic, I can pop over to my friend Franz's palace and thinly lay on the compliments like coats of an at-home gel pedicure. "Oh, YOU always know what to wear and I am like an anorexic Uncle Fester." One movie montage later and I am fully adorned. Gratefully, I return the pumpkin carriage before midnight—usually soaked in ten to twelve pumps of Britney Spears Curious and with a cryptic book of matches left in the breast pocket as if to say "a poor was here."

KATYA:

They say money is the root of all evil. They say money doesn't grow on trees. They also insist that one cannot buy happiness with money, which is excellent news for the poor.

Let's be frank here: Being poor sucks a whole fucking bucket of shit. Contrary to what those Hare Krishnas in Terminal 3 at LAX might tell you, there is no virtue in poverty. Sure, many of us would love to renounce all worldly possessions, take some holy vows, and be whisked off to an austere but fascinating life as a monk in a Buddhist monastery. Who wouldn't? But that's not real life. Real life involves money, and money is what makes the real world go around and around.

I've suffered through many phases of being dirt-ass broke well into my adult years, and up until I was thirty-three years old, I never had more than a thousand dollars in total liquid cash or assets. Those horrifying memories of crippling financial insecurity linger today and allow me to experience deep gratitude for the economic abundance I am currently able to enjoy. Yes, that's right—I am a thousandaire.

I literally have no idea how the economy works. I couldn't even tell you in basic terms what the economy is. The stock market remains an elusive, boring mystery, and I just don't have the energy or interest in learning anything new right now. So that makes me extraqualified to dole out some helpful risk-free financial advice to you, my poor, struggling reader.

1. Build up a three-month emergency fund. I never really had any savings until I was thirty years old. And I definitely didn't have a three-month emergency fund, which is basically enough money for you to live without income for three months. This might seem like a lot, and it is, so don't be discouraged. But it's very important, especially if you're on your own, and Mommy and Daddy aren't around to pay your rent.

2. Save all your change! I have been doing this since I was four years old, and I love it. I even save the pennies, and I separate the quarters for laundry. I love having a big giant container of change; it's very comforting. At the end of the year, I roll up all the change myself (Coinstar takes a percentage) and haul it over to the bank, and then I use the cash to buy lotto tickets!

3. Do not gamble or play the lottery. This is literally wasting your money. You're actually better off just tossing your cash right into the fireplace and it will save you a trip to the store.

4. Explore financial domination! There are plenty of nasty old bankers and lawyers up to their ears in disposable income who are just begging for a lady like you to come around and bully their wallets into submission. This is a form of kink where you, the mistress, get to bully some rich slob into paying your rent, buying your groceries, booking your vacations, etcetera. And the best part? No sex required! Does it sound too good to be true? Well, it probably is, but there's only one way to find out, so let me know how it goes.

5. Let go of the fear of financial insecurity. Remember, there's no amount of money that will ever guarantee us lifelong security, happiness, or peace of mind. We can never truly be free from the possibility of financial hardship, but we can let go of the fear of it. How do we do that? Well, ask yourself, do you have all that you need right now at this moment? If you're reading this book, I'm going to guess that you're not on the street dying of consumption. (If you are, my bad.) Real happiness is found in the moment, not in a future state of wealth. After all, the ultimate indicator of wealth is not cash, stocks, or real estate—it's health! So cheers to you.

YES, I'M

by Katya

PERFECT:
CURATING YOUR
DIGITAL FACADE

Much has already been written about the detrimental effects of social media on the psychosocial development of young people. I'm not particularly keen on adding to the chorus's deafening shrieks warning of the danger of social media and internet addiction. For those smug older folks who are fond of lamenting a bygone era when people were not socially awkward and would engage in meaningful dialogue with strangers instead of staring into their phones, well, I've got news for you: This time never existed for most people, but now we have the benefit of avoiding people with a useful prop and an actual purpose. Not only do the kids of this generation have to weather the rotted hellscape of adolescence in real life; they also must navigate through virtual rings of fire via Snapchat, Instagram, Tinder, Twitter, Facebook, and whatever new interfaces pop up along the way.

Social media is many things, and most of those things are synonyms for "cesspool" or "festering carcass filled with dried shit." I once dated a guy who did not have a Facebook or Instagram account. In fact he had no social media profiles at all—none! We dated for six lovely months before he was convicted of poisoning the water at a middle school in Tampa. Just kidding, but it wouldn't be surprising. He said that when most folks find out he's not online, they assume he's either in the Witness Protection Program or he's just lying. These people with no social media presence are of course extremely rare, and if you're lucky enough to meet one of these gridless ghosts in real life, do check to make sure that it is an actual person and not an Amish specter killing time en route to the next realm.

I am an entertainer and a small-business owner whose primary product is my drag persona, so maintaining a consistent presence on various social media platforms is essential to the health and wealth of KATYA LLC, aka me. And since the horsing around I do online is in the service of my drag character, it's easier to disengage from the phone or computer so I can go live my life as a normal person. For the average girl this can be tricky. Bob Regular and Susie Whatsherface don't have the benefit of funneling all their vanity, selfishness, and brazen sexual impropriety into a marketed fictional presence, so the borders between you and your virtual self can be a lot more porous, and this makes you vulnerable to the many traps embedded in the virtual minefield of the social media landscape.

I'm a passive-aggressive introvert with no boundaries or shame. I cherish my privacy and I guard it fiercely, though I do enjoy the tension of always being under constant threat of a serious breach. I have a lot of experience navigating through life in various modes of notoriety. I got famous (gay-famous) literally overnight, and watched it all play out in real time, hunched over, staring wild-eyed and slack-jawed at my iPhone screen. Before I was swaddled in fame by the greedy exploitative witch claws of reality television, I was just a faceless, nameless zero nothing nobody, just like you, and let me tell you, that was horrible. But when destiny called to tell me that fate was on its way to pick me up to go to dreamland's house, where we were gonna hang out until Opportunity knocked to let us know that Success was pulled up to drive us over to Easy Street, everything changed! As my follower count on all platforms exploded, I sat back and stared at the digital carnage in ravenous delight. And in the weeks that followed, people around me noticed a remarkable shift in my personality, most notably the fact that it didn't exist: I had become a withered husk of a person gazing mutely at his phone in a near constant state of glassy-eyed catatonia.

Whether you're promoting your new exercise equipment, hawking knives for a pyramid scheme, staffing your German hip-hop yoga retreat, stalking an ex-boyfriend, or reinvigorating your love of cyberbullying, let's take a look at some ways to make the most out of social media and avoid the seemingly inevitable erosion of your once fun and affable personality.

The first general rule is simple and it's one that hopefully all of us were taught in kindergarten: Don't be a goddamn rude-ass piece-of-shit fuck-face bitch. Or, in the queen's English: Kindness is key. Listen, there's a reason all those adages persist long after childhood, and the simplest ones are usually the most important. We don't often have the luxury of meticulously curating the events of our lives in the real world, so it can be a lot more difficult to be a radiant source of divine light when that fat bitch Karen from marketing takes a shit in the break room fridge (again!). But you certainly don't need to follow her on Facebook, because you know very well that you're going to leave a string of nasty messages on her timeline underneath a photo of her face edited onto a dead cow. I am generally pretty consistent when it comes to the airing of grievances online: Unless it's intended solely for the purpose of entertaining my fans, I'll keep my shitty comment to myself and scream at my friends on the phone about it like a normal person. Another benefit of avoiding negativity online is that when that pyramid scheme finally pays off and you're a famous Tuvan throat singer, you won't have to worry about getting kicked out of show business by haters dredging up your old racist tweets.

The next tip is simple: Take a moment and delete any old racist tweets. It's okay, nobody's perfect, and we all grow and change. A good digital housecleaning is in order from time to time, and even if we have no intentions of becoming a ruthless politician or a widely celebrated entertainer, a consistent sweep of the online broom keeps our little social media nest free and clear of bullshit. Plus, it can be very enlightening to revisit some entries in our digital diaries to observe just how far we've grown and developed as a person, or in most cases just to remember what we ate for lunch one day five years ago in spectacularly unnecessary detail.

Other people can't be counted on to do the same, though, so let's kick some of the shitheads out of your digital block party. One thing I used to find myself doing at three in the morning is following these horrifying threads of conservative pundits on Twitter and obsessively poring over feuds, fights, and generally scum-laden trash heaps of ignorant right-wing vitriol. The social media landscape is a 24/7 all-access provider of every conceivable car-crash scenario, and it is our job to yank our eyeballs away from the carnage. I recall many times having finally put the phone down after thoroughly surveying the stupidity online, fully convinced that I would wake up the next day with a lower IQ score. So it's helpful and wildly beneficial for the brain, body, and eyeballs to diligently apply some self-inflicted guidelines if you are like me, prone to obsessive bouts of marathon media consumption.

MUTE IS A MIRACLE, BLOCK IS A BLESSING.

—MOTHER TERESA

A general rule that is excellent and must be strictly adhered to for maximum benefit: no phone in the bed, ever. I use the alarm on my phone to wake up, so I keep it near my bed but switch it to airplane mode so no one can disturb my much-needed beauty rest. People in my life know that if there is an emergency, I'm not the one you call for help. If it has to do with me directly, it can wait until morning. The only way I am being shaken from slumber to deal with a matter directly is if there is a murderer who has broken into my apartment and is about to kill me, and even then, ugh, just hurry up and get it over with; I'm tired and my legs hurt.

That's the tea. No need to target, menace, or bully. No need to scream-cry into the void or hurl invectives at the ether. You see a dumbass cunt or some gross piece-of-shit dude, simply block 'em and keep on steppin'. No need to respond to their misguided ploys for attention every single day with the same witty retort, because they're not going to learn, you're not going to grow, and, Deborah, ain't nobody going to change for the better. Just hack that brush with your online machete and clear up the digital path for your followers so you can all go peacefully into the night to enjoy a steamy discussion at the Harry Styles lesbian fan fic world headquarters.

What happens if you wake up one day, start scrolling through your feed, and realize, "Oh wow, all my friends on here are either boring, stupid, annoying, or all three"? Mute them! People of this ilk are likely to notice you blocking or unfollowing them, as they likely do not have joy in their life to distract them from such banal trivialities, so go ahead and silently smash the mute button and rid your TL of their tedious, rambling nonsense.

Also, if you subscribe to one of those astrology websites that posts on your behalf every single day, flooding the internet with random, unsolicited astrological advice, you should be blocked from participating in any form of social media and then incarcerated in a minimum-security prison for at least three years. You know who you are, so click here to read more daily forecast for Gemini.

Here's a little story before my last tip. A couple of years ago, I went completely bat-shit-bananas-out-of-my-mind crazy. During a moment of particularly delusional paranoia, I became convinced that my phone was the conduit of malevolent energetic forces perpetrated by a shadowy government agency that were steadily poisoning my brain. So I threw my phone across the street into the woods and with a sigh of relief began the fifteen-minute walk to my friend's house, which turned into about three hours of getting lost because I couldn't remember the address and had no way to check, because I threw my phone into the woods. But I gotta say, despite actually being full-tilt insane at the time, those three hours away from the phone felt so refreshing, so unencumbered and unburdened. It was incredible to consider what a constant, powerful connection to the digital realm I had, and 90 percent of it was social media. Long story short, every once in a while, put the phone down.

One of the main features of social media is allowing the world to see all the interesting activities and relationships that make up your very fascinating and unique life. But what if all your life consists of is hours and hours of mindlessly scrolling through social media and the only interesting thing about you is that your skin hasn't fused to the furniture in your apartment? Well, Claire, it's time to get up and out of the house and experience the full depth and breadth of that vivid and exciting thing we call life. I've made a list of some real-life experiences that cannot be shared on social media but will certainly enrich your physical life in real time, as well as provide excellent fodder for a future autobiography.

1. Get in bed with the Mafia. An underground crime syndicate is a great place to explore the full spectrum of the human experience, while maintaining privacy in the cozy underbelly of an illegal and dangerous shadowy netherworld.

2. Get in bed with the Amish. Sure, it may be kinda hacky to throw it back and trade in the phone for a potato sack, but there's no faster way to learn the true value of the human condition than embracing an ascetic, electricity-free farmer's lifestyle. Wagon Wheel Watusi—go!

3. Get in bed with an undercover double agent working for a shadowy organized crime syndicate who's planning on infiltrating a secret sect of radicalized Amish terrorists. Need I say more?

INTERIOR DESIGN:

by Trixie

SHOW ME YOUR INSIDES

Shortly after closing on my condo in Hollywood, I did a detailed walk-through of my new place: the view of the Hollywood sign, the high ceilings, and an open floor plan that offered a great raw space. However, the fixtures were dated, the appliances were cheap, and the putrid orange kitchen floor looked like that of an abandoned Baja Fresh.

Living in an unappealing space can feel like being trapped under a vending machine. As strangers swarm the scene and your life leaves your body, you remember the worst part of the situation: You're out one dollar and you never got your airport Nutter Butter. But there is a way to save the dollar AND get the Nutter Butter: embracing the transformative magic of interior design.

Think of interior design as putting your home in drag. Four white walls? That might be okay for a mental health facility, but we don't live in mental health facilities. (Okay, clearly, some of us do.) Imagine being at a drag show with all the whip cracks, cartwheel splits, and drink specials but with NO DRAG. Then it's just a thirty-five-year-old bald guy lip-syncing to "My Heart Will Go On" in Russian, and no one wants that. (Okay, clearly, some of us do.)

There's no handbook to home decor the same way there's no handbook to life (except for this one). But there are no spaces that can't be improved by paint, pillows, and personality. That's why I sought counsel from my elderly gay roommate, who has worked as an interior designer for several decades. He allowed me to interview him in our dining room while wearing a collection of bangles and a headscarf.

"YOUR HOME SHOULD NEVER BE LOUDER THAN YOU ARE"

Okay, taken literally, this also makes sense. If you can't hear your own conversation above your radiator or toilet, you probably need to make a call to maintenance. Or perhaps your design problems are supernatural in nature.

But it also means that you should find a way to decorate your home that supports you instead of competes with you. If you're a person who sells religious novels door to door, a shag carpet isn't for you. Neither is a bold wallpaper. Try a dusty wooden drawing figure and a rotary phone that doesn't work. Or get a real job.

"ALL CHAIR LEGS SHOULD BE ENTIRELY ON A RUG OR ENTIRELY OFF"

Now, this might seem psychotic. You're probably thinking, "Trixie, you've gone too far! You're beautiful but fascist." Well, you're half-right. Having furniture legs on and off rugs tells visitors, "I don't know where I am but I'm barely hanging on." If that is the story you'd like to tell, there are more compelling ways to unravel. (See: drugs.)

Again, I know this rule sounds crazy. But now that I've planted the seed, every unbalanced rug placement will send you into a full-tilt *Mommie Dearest* "wire hangers" tirade. You're welcome!

"DON'T OVER-THEME"

You don't deserve this. You did not purchase a lifestyle book written by a famous drag queen duo to have them police your thematic instincts. But let me tell you, it's fun to choose a theme. A little design narrative or story line can really set the tone of a room. I have a unicorn statue near my bed and hooved feet on my bench at the foot of my bed, as if to say, "Nothing about sleeping with me will feel real, but it will be a great story."

It's one thing to suggest a feeling or an idea with your decor. It's quite another to wrench your guest by the senses and force them to know that your kitchen theme is "roosters." Or your bathroom theme is "seahorses." Nailing ceramic seahorses all over your bathroom does not make your bathroom "themed." It makes your bathroom gross—like you moved into a Long John Silver's and changed nothing.

"HANG ART AT EYE LEVEL"

But everyone is a different height! Even Trixie can deviate in height depending on the size of the heel and the height of the hair. I think it's safe to pick around five ten—a little higher if you have high ceilings. No one should have to crane their neck to see your framed Tammie Brown used makeup wipe.

People under five ten really shouldn't be in your house to begin with. They don't have much to offer in the way of hired help or meaningful relationships.

IN CONCLUSION

At the end of the day, you have to follow your artistic voice. If your heart is telling you to hang a framed poster that says EAT, LOVE, INSPIRE in your kitchen, go for it. Just also know that your guests will JUDGE, STARE, AND IMMEDIATELY LEAVE.

FOOD :

THE FOOD PYRAMID SCHEME

THREE CULINARY SUGGESTIONS
BY TRIXIE AND KATYA

TRIXIE:

You can't outrun a bad diet." Six-year-old me also couldn't outrun a rogue bottle rocket in 1995, but we won't be addressing the ethics of fireworks until our next book, *Paris Is Actually Burning: Celebrating the Fourth of July in the Gay Club.*

Food is organized in a pyramid for a reason: because it is sacred. And just like abusing a pyramid, abusing food can lead to complications, including but not limited to a mummy's reanimation.

Personally, I can't be trusted with food. If left at a restaurant alone, I will order one of everything on the menu, mix it into a giant bowl, and crawl inside the way an old man would enter a Jacuzzi: slow but relaxed. I could eat pizza and ice cream for every meal for every day for the rest of my life. The problem is my Wisconsin DNA knows that I'm thirty—and it knows what's next. My body is like, "Shouldn't we have front rolls by now? Or at least a bum knee and a wandering eye?"

So, I read a lot of *Men's Health* magazine. Not just so I have access to hot pictures of John Krasinski reflecting on his full-body transformation for an acting role, but so I can learn by osmosis what it is hot people eat. My top two:

QUINOA

I was once on a photo shoot for a high-end vodka campaign. I was feeling tight, thin, and ready to get a little drunk on set. We took a break for lunch and I slipped into my terry-cloth robe before approaching the lunch table. A lunch table in Los Angeles will offer basic greens and small plates of prepared health food. My assistant, bless her heart, walked up to the table and said, "What is this?" The craft services person said with absolute bewilderment and disbelief, "It's quinoa." You could feel a room full of superhot advertising and film people screech to a halt. Shamed and belittled, my assistant scuttled to the dressing room, never to be seen again.

CELERY JUICE

Have you ever wanted to have juice but also not enjoy it whatsoever? A sizable bottle of celery juice will only set you back ten calories! You'll feel thin, hungry, and nauseated. It's the type of beverage you drink publicly and when someone notices, you say dismissively, "Oh, thanks, it's supposed to be really good for you." Celery juice strengthens the bones, purifies the bloodstream, and heals the guts—basically it will keep you alive. Unfortunately, the taste of celery juice will make you want to die.

KATYA:

One of my most enduring personality quirks is that I hate food and pretty much always have. I am an extremely picky eater with an embarrassingly long and annoying list of ingredients that will render a meal inedible to me. I hate almost every type of sandwich because I find most American lunch foods disgusting—every type of cheese served cold (I'll only eat mozzarella on a pizza); every type of condiment, like relish, mayo, mustard (ketchup is fine for French fries)—and I absolutely loathe eating anything that comes from the ocean.

I have fantasized about a food pill for much of my life, one that I could just pop down with a glass of water, and voilà! Eight hundred to twelve hundred calories of fortifying nutrition would dissolve and spread throughout my body while I could occupy myself with other more interesting activities.

There have been years when I have basically lived off of everything bagels (with butter only—cream cheese might as well be congealed bird shit to me), coffee, and Indian food. I have never learned to cook, and at the time of writing this I have ordered the same Indian takeout three to five times a week for the past year (chicken vindaloo, basmati rice, and garlic naan). When I find something I like, I tend to ride that wagon 'til the wheels fall off.

I know a great many people struggle with food, overeating, dieting, and weight loss. I could eat twenty pounds of chocolate cake and thirty pounds of ice cream and not gain a damn ounce. Thanks to genetics, weird taste buds, and an outrageously overzealous metabolism, I've never had to struggle with my weight. (My battle tends to involve a chemical component—see the drugs chapter.)

The only times I have ever consistently prepared a nutritious and satisfying meal that tasted delicious was when I was doing yoga teacher training back in Boston. I was in excellent shape, I wasn't smoking cigarettes, and I would pop out of bed each morning to prepare my favorite meal of the day: breakfast.

To be fair, I can't in all honesty say I hate food, because I fucking love breakfast, and to me as an American, breakfast is a mostly sweet rather than savory affair. I simply must have something sweet upon waking, which proves a bit tricky when traveling abroad—places like China and Brazil don't really do sweet breads, pastries, or cakes in the morning. Call me crazy, but I've just never been able to pop out of bed in the morning and eat a lasagna. It just feels wrong.

STEEL-CUT OATMEAL WITH LOTS OF TASTY SHIT IN IT

Cooking steel-cut oats kinda takes a while—usually around thirty minutes—so it's best to cook up a big batch all at once to last you through most of the week. I would prepare it on Sunday night and then store the cooked oatmeal in a large Tupperware container in the fridge. Each morning I carve out a portion and heat it up in the microwave with some half-and-half or whole milk. Then, my personal love affair with all things sugar would commence as I would add a tablespoon (or two) of brown sugar, followed by fresh raspberries, fresh blueberries, fresh strawberries, sometimes a Medjool date to get wild. Then for texture, crunch, and protein, throw in a teaspoon or two of chia seeds, a handful of chopped walnuts and/or cashews, or some granola. At one point I tried to cut down on sugar so I replaced the brown sugar with agave syrup, but then I would end up adding honey, which led me back to the brown sugar. Some folks like a pat of butter in there or even ghee (clarified butter). After all this shit is added you should have a pretty sizable bowl, and let me tell you, this breakfast is goddamn delicious, nutritious, and the best kind of fuel to start your day. You can also sneak some weird healthfoody type supplements in here like whatever snake oil du jour Goop is hawking, and you won't even notice its nasty flavor.

So that's it! My masterclass in gastronomy is about as exciting as one would expect from a thirty-seven-year-old white American druggie. Oatmeal in the morning, a pack of smokes for lunch, and a luxurious dinner of chicken, rice, and unleavened garlic bread. Bon appétit and good-bye.

TRAVEL:

WHEREVER YOU GO, THERE YOU ARE

a CONVERSATION
with TRIXIE and KATYA

"TRIXIE: I love to *travèl* . . . No, actually, I don't. Let me tell you about traveling: It sounds enjoyable, until you do it all the time.**"**

129

K: Yes, I agree. I remember distinctly there was a period in my life when I felt so ashamed that I hadn't traveled a lot, because to me the coolest thing was not being rich or being sexy; it was to be a world traveler.

T: To casually be like, "Oh, I just got back from Milan."

K: I felt like I hadn't lived, and I felt the economic barrier between me and that experience was so vast and that I was never going to be able to be cool, because I was never going to be able to travel. And then . . . come to find out . . . it's rotten. I mean, it's not rotten.

T: For me, it is a status thing, and it's an economic thing, because when you're okey-smokey-pokey from the country-untry, you go down to the Walmart and come home. You buy school clothes once a year, and that's your trip. Versus, like, to be one of those people who not only travels, but is like, "Ugh, it's so exhausting . . . Ugh, I have to go again next week." Like, last fall I was in New York for DragCon; then I flew back to LA; then I flew back to New York again. And that's the first time I'd ever flown to New York like two weeks in a row. I was like, "What career would be worth this?"

K: I don't know . . . I mean. This one!

T: Yeah! I guess being a celebrated author.

K: So, the traveling lifestyle can take many different shapes. For starters, you have the businessman.

T: Those are the ones I feel bad for, because they are traveling in suits. And sometimes they are not traveling with suitcases because they fly in that morning and fly home that night.

K: They're lucky if they get three scotch and sodas at the hotel bar and then a quick yank in the bathroom.

T: Those businessmen are the drinkers!

K: Yes! Seven a.m.! Bloody Mary!

T: I was on a flight once and the guy wanted a drink, and it was a five thirty a.m. boarding time, and they can't serve booze until six a.m. on flights. This guy was *plucked* that it was five thirty a.m. and he couldn't get a fucking drink. If you could have seen me crack my neck when this guy was like, "What?" and I was like, "Well, it's also five thirty, you *psycho*. By the way, you're in a suit, you're obviously going somewhere important. Unless you think the plane's going down and you're just trying to dress for the funeral."

K: I've been on at least two flights where I was the only fag in first class, and everybody was drinking in the morning. Every guy was drinking a gin and tonic, Bloody Mary, scotch and soda, whatever. Everybody was drinking. At like seven in the morning!

T: The only flights I drink on are the very long ones. Like ten, eleven hours. Like, here to London? You have your little two drinks, maybe with your dinner, and then lie down, because it kind of makes you go to sleep.

K: You take a pill?

T: No, but, like, two drinks for me will do it.

K: I sort of envy the people who can take a pill.

T: You can't take a pill?

K: No, I can't take a pill. Because it's all narcotics.

T: You can't even take an over-the-counter sleeping pill?

K: No, technically I could do that.

T: Like those gummies?

K: I would need a horse tranquilizer. Come on!

T: "Hi, miss? Could you go down to Economy Comfort Plus and hit me with this crowbar? But surprise me because I don't like pain." Back to people who drink on the plane: There's something about being in the air that I think makes you drunker?

K: Maybe the altitude? Cabin pressure?

T: And because you're seated and the plane's kind of moving, you can't really tell you're drunk. Until you arrive somewhere and you're borderline hungover.

K: Yeah, and then you have to be poured off the plane.

T: Also, whenever I get off a plane, my skin truly feels dehydrated, covered with a swampy film.

K: I feel like scum. Slimy, oily scum. It's disgusting. What about etiquette on a plane? I've been seeing a lot of pictures of people with bare feet on the wall, or on the seat in front of them.

T: Bitch. Also, wear socks. You cannot wear sandals on a plane. This isn't your fucking house.

K: Yeah, that would also be a rookie mistake in the summer. Because it's actually freezing in the plane.

T: I think the ideal travel outfit would be either a stretchy jean, a thin, stretchy jean, or, like . . . a jogger.

K: Like, a dressier jogger! Not like shit-stained sweats with holes in it. Also, please shower!

T: Did I ever tell you about the time the girl pissed her pants on my flight?

K: What?!

T: Yes. You won't believe it. This is back when I was flying economy. So I'm in the middle seat, this bitch is in the middle seat on the other side. And we're taking off in the plane, and she's rocking back and forth. And I'm thinking, like, "Oh, she's fucking scared to fly. Maybe she's freaking out." Middle seat, she's probably not an experienced traveler. And then I smell . . . piss. And while we're on the incline, she has pissed herself, pissed into the bucket of the seat, pissed down her legs, and the pee has hit the ground and traveled back. So then she gets up, piss all over her pants. I'm staring at her piss. And then she reaches into the overhead, goes into her bag, pulls out everything to find a little pair of jeans, goes to the bathroom, changes pants, puts her pissy pants back in her fucking bag, and gets the flight attendant to walk by and give everyone in the row behind her free chips. "I noticed you're covered in piss, have some Fritos."

K: Wow.

T: Also, we have talked about this to no end: If it's not your boarding group—

K: SIT. THE. FUCK. DOWN. SIT THE FUCK DOWN!

T: We're all getting on a plane.

K: The only somewhat logical thing I've noticed people get really stressed out about is being able to stow their bags in the overhead compartment.

T: They'll check it for free if it doesn't fit! Who fucking cares?

K: Yes. It is so crazy to me. People are just dying to get on that plane and sit there.

T: To do nothing. In my opinion, first class should board last.

K: Last! And then get off first!

T: Yes, I want to spend less time on the plane.

K: I've been so tired, for a long time I was traveling that hectic schedule of club gigs, and if I had an early flight I would stay up all night. So I'd be on the plane exhausted. But there was one time in South America that I was so tired, and I was in first class with all these Spanish businessmen, and my mouth . . . I was writhing around, apparently, in the chair and drooling, snoring with my mouth wide-open. It was so embarrassing.

T: When I first did *Drag Race*, the first few gigs afterward, the adrenaline of being able to perform and travel keeps you going.

K: Yup! The whole first year.

T: The adrenaline of like . . . Oh God, I'm in Dallas tonight, tomorrow I'm in Seattle, then I have a Pride in Miami! Your first Pride season being famous, you're like, "Fuck sleep! I can party all night." And then it turns into "If I can't get the full sleep I'm a zombie at the gig." In that first year, I remember staying up, having drinks at the bar, getting out of drag at three, and I had to be at the airport at six. In that situation, you're like, why would I go to sleep? What is two hours? That's worse?

K: Yeah, that is worse, because your body gets a taste of it and then the stress of oversleeping or missing the alarm is not worth it.

T: I have done the thing where I lie down in my outfit I'm going to the airport in. So I can just stand up and leave.

K: I read somewhere that the best advice for packing is to wait one hour before you have to leave to the airport. Sounds stressful, but I actually do that by default because I'm lazy. And it works because you just take the essentials!

T: That is the tea. My boyfriend, who I bring on trips sometimes, he'll spend a day packing.

K: Seventeen kimonos.

T: He'll do all the laundry in his house and then spend a whole day. And then every time he takes everything out and repacks the bag before we go to the airport. What kind of lifestyle is that? I swear to God, I was in San Francisco a little while ago for a gig, and I didn't even bring clean underwear or socks. Who gonna check me, boo? Who gonna check me, boo?

K: Speaking of checking, at TSA I got the full pat-down a little while ago. The full fantasy. They asked if I wanted to go into a private room, and I was like, "No, no, that's all right," and then I realized why they ask you that: They go in and they get *thorough*. The guy was not even attractive and I got fully erect. Because he groped my genitals! He touched my dick and balls and ass. My whole ass.

T: I flew without my ID once, and they had to give me the full pat-down. And I remember it happened in front of Willam, and Willam was taking videos and, like, zooming in on me saying I was a terrorist . . . which I was.

K: I'm gonna fly without my ID sometimes.
Just for a little human connection.

T: The entire TSA is performative. If you have a gun? You're not carrying it on, Catherine! It's to make the passengers feel that something's happening. The plane is not safer, I'm sorry. Can I have a bottle of water on the fucking plane?

K: No, you cannot. But you can bring a gun into a Walmart. Like, what the fuck is that?

T: Have you ever seen an attentive TSA agent? It's always some girl, like, "What time are you off tomorrow? I'm off tonight. We're going to see *The Lion King*." They're passing your assault rifle through. "Yeah, Beyoncé is in *Lion King*."

K: Speaking of which, do you get all bent out of shape about people traveling like Boo Boo the Fool in terms of their outfits and stuff? Like, why don't you just dress up? Everyone's wearing pajamas and stuff.

T: No, I don't think you should wear pajamas. You're, like, a grown woman wearing SpongeBob pajamas at the airport . . . I hope your plane goes down. I have an airplane outfit: black joggers, a black track jacket or hoodie, black baseball cap, a black T-shirt—I paint my legs black. I just want something that is comfortable, but black still looks nice. I don't know. I'm trying to be invisible. I get recognized at the airport less and less nowadays, which I love.

KATYA: The best thing is, I've never felt more invisible than when I've been traveling with Detox. She pulls ALL the focus. She'll be wearing like a Keith Haring matching neon Gucci sweat suit. "

T: With a neon-yellow bowl cut, wearing big sunglasses. And she'll go to the TSA agent, like, "How you doing today, boyfriend?"

K: With her twelve-inch-long acrylic nails. Yeah, I've never felt more invisible. It's great.

T: I will say, the idea of having time off and going somewhere makes me sick. The willful trip I'll make once a year is to go home for Christmas. Or Palm Springs, which is like a two-hour drive. But if you were going to, where would you go? Didn't you go to Thailand?

K: I went to fucking Thailand! Alone. My stupid ass went for two weeks. And no smoking, because it was a yoga retreat center.

T: Were you, like, smoking in secret?

K: Mary, I had to walk a half a mile down the dirt road in the blazing-hot sun to find a piece of shade where I could smoke in private. Like, literally hiding. And then one day the yoga teacher retreat leaders came walking down the street, and they saw me and they said, "Namaste," and I almost cried.

T: 'Cause you felt exposed?

K: Exposed and dragged. I was a fraud. And I had to take four fucking planes to get there! It was awful.

T: We travel enough that we are comfortable. Some people are nervous travelers.

K: That I don't get. What is there to be nervous about? Everything is taken care of. You just have to show up. And if anything goes wrong, it's completely out of your control. Were you ever afraid of flying?

T: When I first started traveling I was a little, but the more I did . . . the odds are so against the plane going down. And if it does, I deserved it. You know what I mean? Like if this plane goes down, if I'm one in a million, I did something.

K: Also, again with statistics, you are definitely going to die. Thank God!

T: I love the idea that you have to put the tray up. You think this tray is going to threaten my life? I'll break it.

K: I recently learned that you can't have a laptop in the seat pouch because if that thing flies out it could decapitate somebody. Think about it! The plane stopping real short. Scalped, snatched bald.

T: It should be safe for flying—it is called a MacBook *Air*. I had an Uber driver once who was a flight attendant. I was like, "Give me the tea, why do we put the seat up?" He said, it's because when the seat is reclined it's locked. When it's up, it has some give. It's meant to support your head. I think I'm so resolute that, if the plane goes down, we are going to die. There is no chance you can live.

K: But more importantly, you can't do anything about it.

T: If you got hit by a car, you could maybe, like, brace yourself. That plane is going down?

K: You can't control that!

T: You might as well get to know your neighbor. Oh my God, I was on a flight recently flying back to LA and I heard the people behind me go, "Roger? Dan." and I was like, who introduces themselves on a plane?

K: We're not at church.

T: Have you ever cried on a plane? I've cried for a while on planes.

K: Over WHAT?

T: It was a dark, deep patch. I was choking on my tears. And this little girl next to me went, "Are you okay?"

K: That is so sad!

T: Yeah . . .

K: Have you ever jerked off on a plane?

T: No. It's never been that deep. Also, I don't feel sexy on a plane, but I do get boners.

K: Yeah, it's boner city on a plane.

T: But it's air boners. It's not like sexy boners. None of these flight attendants are ever hot. Why do gay guys always want to be flight attendants? Is that glamorous to us? Do you think when we're kids we see them in their uniform and we're like, "That is glamorous, I want to be that"?

K: I don't know. Traveling the world is definitely glamorous.

T: Especially some of those outfits! The Virgin Australia girls? Are serving. The makeup? The Virgin Australia girls have makeup–LASHES! The side bun with the ascot? And those international planes have a bar. We were on a flight to Dubai once, and there was a full bar-lounge. It was Emirates.

K: Emirates was my most luxurious flight experience ever.

T: Did you take a shower on the plane?

K: I took *two* showers. The bathroom was bigger than the one in my apartment. And at the beginning of the flight, they came—I swear to God I had like three dedicated air stewardesses—and said, "Would you like to schedule a shower?" I said, "Absolutely I would," and she gave me a tour of it. She chirped "So at twenty-five minutes a red light will go on, indicating there are five minutes of water left." You can take a thirty-fucking-minute shower on that goddamn plane.

T: Where's the water coming from?

K: From the showerhead? I don't know. The fish tank in the trunk of the plane.

T: Moving on: hotels.

K: I love hotels. Obviously I love a fancy one, and I've had the opportunity to stay in some fancy ones. But I love any hotel.

T: Me too, bitch! I get the best sleep of my life.

K: I don't think I've ever had a bad night's sleep at a hotel.

T: Give me a sixty-one-degree room.

K: Yes! Stiff, white cardboard sheets.

T: Let me take a shower that's so hot that I am pinked. My feet are red. And let me put on a free robe. A free robe with a free slipper.

K: Oh yeah. I will use seven towels in one night. I don't know why! Seven towels in one night!

T: I will wipe shit on that towel.

K: If you don't travel a lot, and this is something that's really important, you must leave a tip for housekeeping. You must. Ninety-nine percent of the time I remember. And I have a tendency to overtip, especially because of the amount I'm getting paid to be there. And then I think about all the work they do, because I've worked in hotels.

T: You have?

K: Yeah, I worked as a busboy at a restaurant in a Holiday Inn, bitch. It was really hard work, and I did room service. I brought up the trays to the rooms.

T: You used to go up to people's rooms? What did you feel like when you walked in?

K: Every time I prayed that it was gonna be a hot, sexy guy—his robe was gonna open, and I was gonna go in there and blow him.

T: Do you know how many times I've had room service delivered to me when I'm in half drag?

K: Oh sure! What do they say, anything?

T: Nothing. They act like it's normal, which is weirder. Don't act like every order you've delivered tonight is for fucking scalped Marge Simpson answering the door. I'd love it if they were like [moans] but it never happens. Monique Heart just told me an Uber driver was like, "Yeah, you wanna rub my shoulders?" That never happens to me!

K: It happens—not in Ubers, but it happened to me a lot in cabs.

T: This is what happens to me in Ubers. They drive by, see me in drag, and keep driving, and they cancel the ride. Maybe it hasn't happened to you because with your drag, maybe it's too late. You're already stepping in the car before they realize something's going on. But my fuckin' ass?

K: Bozo the Clown. This is no clown car.

T: Is that an oil painting of Jennifer Coolidge waiting for the bus? Yeah, they've driven by. God, I take so many Ubers. My tax guy told me the dollar amount I'd spent on Ubers. It was like thirty thousand dollars.

K: Holy shit!

T: Uber's really changed the game for travel.

K: It's completely changed the game. I don't have a car in LA. And I live a wonderful life.

T: *You* live a wonderful life?

K: One thing that I still have such a hard time understanding is why people continue to have that irrational fear of flying and ignore the very rational fear of driving.

T: Tea! When you hear the statistics of flying and then you hear that driving is worse, it makes driving seem like a suicide pact.

K: Would you say you're a good traveler?

T: I would say I'm a calm traveler. I use the sky lounge every time I travel, and that's definitely a game changer. Because remember all the time you'd spend sitting out in the open at airports?

K: Like a dusty old rube.

T: Yes, and if you have any kind of fame, the Sky Club is kind of a shelter. Girl, I have woken up hungover and still drunk, rolled into the lounge, and showered. Taken a nice cold shower at the airport.

K: I will never forget the feeling of deplaning that Emirates freshly showered.

T: Did you feel like Jennifer–

K: Aniston! Absolutely I did, it was the strangest experience to exit the plane cleaner than when I got on it. I would say I'm a good traveler because I have master control over my bowel movements. Master control. I remember I was in high school and went to France for my first big international trip.

T: Did you buy leather pants?

K: I sure did. Every international trip I buy leather pants. I was with my friend Dave, I spoke excellent French, and he . . . did not really. And we were exploring on our own and he had to pee. Really badly. And there's nowhere to piss. He was begging me to ask somebody to use the bathroom and I was like, I don't know where. And I'm just thinking, oh my God, how sad for you. He can't hold his pee anymore.

T: For you, it's like, "I gotta pee, so I have until tomorrow."

K: What's your favorite mode of transportation?

T: Not gonna lie, I live for a train. First class on a train? They feed you, there's Wi-Fi.

K: Yeah, it's cool! But not if you have a lot of luggage.

T: Not cool. But they also don't charge for luggage. I mean, trains run on time, and you can get there two minutes before.

K: Yeah, that's true.

T: I love that about trains. And if you miss it, there's probably another one in an hour.

K: Yeah.

T: What do you like? I hate road trips, bitch.

K: I don't live for a road trip. I am the worst navigator. You give me Google Maps? I will get us lost. And then I'm a terrible driver to boot, so it's a lose-lose for all involved.

T: Do you have a license still?

K: Yeah, I do . . . It might be expired, though. And if I'm in the passenger seat, I'll fall asleep immediately.

T: We should do a travel movie. A road movie in the style of *To Wong Foo* and *The Adventures of Priscilla, Queen of the Desert* where you and I are traveling because I'm going to meet my real dad for the first time, and you're going to a meet and greet with Julia Roberts.

K: And we don't know how we're going to get there. And there's a moment where the car breaks down and to get the money to fix the carburetor we have to win a drag show.

T: But we go there like it's going to be fine, and it's an amateur drag show where everyone's incredible, and we have to try to win.

K: What would we call it?

T: *To Priscilla, Thanks for Nothing, Julia Roberts.*

DECLUTTERING YOUR CONDO, MARIE

by Trixie

The only thing I love more than collecting tons of bizarre, useless decorative objects is throwing them in the garbage when their charm has worn off! Whether it's a good old spring-cleaning in the garage or a much-needed purge of your sycophantic entourage, the process of decluttering can be tough, but ultimately it is exhilarating. My mother has always been my role model in this department, especially in our home growing up, as we all had a tendency to acquire lots of shit. Weekly purges would occur unannounced, and anything and everything you might have left around the kitchen or living room was likely to be chucked into the bin. I share a similar attitude and I take great pleasure in clearing out unnecessary debris, although with drag it can be particularly difficult.

Let's start with your physical environment. Are you a hoarder? Do you struggle to let go of items in the hope that they might one day become useful, no matter how useless and bizarre they might be? Do you find it difficult to part with your stacks and stacks of *Boston Globe* newspapers that date back to 1983? And what about those dozens of Nalgene bottles filled with your "summer urine" you've been collecting for the last ten years? Not to mention the tower of empty CD cases that stretches all the way to the lofted ceiling. If this sounds familiar, then you, my friend, have a wonderfully exciting mental health journey to embark on. Take the quiz to learn how far gone you are:

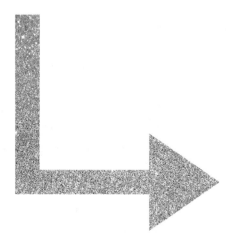

Quiz: Am I a collector or a hoarder?

When someone brings up hoarding, I:

a) FEEL VERY ATTACKED!

b) refer to a favorite reality show on hoarding.

c) climb my dirty-diaper mountain in my living room—I can't hear that right now.

In my den, I have:

a) a showcase of bicentennial stamps.

b) a charred Princess Diana Beanie Baby.

c) not been able to enter my den in years.

I love pets. I have:

a) two terriers, Brooke Lynn and Miss Vanjie.

b) pets are dirty, but I love a bird feeder.

c) seventy-one cats and four skeletons.

When I don't want something, I:

a) donate it to a women's shelter.

b) keep it—I might need it!

c) Every item has a memory attached and it has driven my family out of my life entirely.

If you tried to remove things from my home, I:

a) have no emotional attachment to objects.

b) would fall apart momentarily, but I would graciously recover.

c) THOSE DEAD PLANTS HAVE MEMORIES.

Finally, when I need to purge, I start with:

a) mismatched socks and Tupperware lids.

b) mountains of California Raisins memorabilia.

c) friendships with those who say I "have too much stuff." BEAT IT! And don't touch my dead plants on the way out!

If you answered mostly Cs (honestly, any amount of C answers is concerning), you are probably a hoarder—but don't worry. Having mental illness is like having a short torso or a big forehead—there are ways around it. Here's my foolproof plan to decluttering:

HIRE SOMEONE

I grew up extremely poor. I learned how to be very self-sufficient and handle everything on my own. Then in my midtwenties, I became rich and famous and my entire sense of self-sufficiency shifted. TaskRabbit or an out-of-work-actor friend became my personal staffing solution. The advantage here of having a second pair of hands is the blindness. I will fight you to the death for a five-year-old pair of wrongly sized shoes from Primark that I never wear. But if my assistant throws them away and doesn't tell me, I never realize they're gone or ever even think of them again. If my husband ever dies prematurely, just remove the body and his belongings from my home—I bet I'd completely forget I was ever married.

YELL FROM ANOTHER ROOM

If you're only lightly involved in your own problems, like me, you can let your TaskRabbit or teenage child worker describe items to you vaguely via Skype while you lounge in another part of the house. I pull out my earbuds only long enough to scream, "Keep" or "Toss."

KEEP GOING

Sure you've eliminated all of your unworn clothes and excess tchotchkes, but why stop there? Pick up every single item in your house with your hands, close your eyes, and think, "Is this something I need to survive?" Daily insulin? Gone! Toothbrush—for what, for me? For society? No. Vitamin C's 1999 single "Graduation" on compact disc? KEEP, bitch.

LEAVE ROOM FOR JESUS

The most valuable thing I've picked up is to end every purge leaving room for more stuff. You're going to get fifteen to twenty Tamagotchis as gifts at the

meet and greet, and when they all start beeping on the same feeding cycle, you will be happy you have an unclaimed drawer to stuff them in until they die.

IN CONCLUSION

People are like goldfish: We naturally expand to the size of our fishbowls. If you're going to become an old fag who owns thirty to forty giant wigs, you'd better hope you have a three-bedroom penthouse unit to store them in.

Truthfully, like what you like and don't feel bad about it. I can't stand having too many pieces of furniture in a small room, but apparently literally hundreds of dolls in my home don't bother me.

RELATI

PART THREE

ONSHIPS

MEETING PEOPLE:

CHARMED, I'M SURE

TIPS FROM TRIXIE AND KATYA

TRIXIE:

I once read an article on Science.com (yes, that's real) that informed me that when you track people's locations by their cell phone signals, it is revealed that most people go to the same three to five places every single day. Home, work, gym, etcetera. The routes stay the same, the people interacted with stay the same, and the routine is invariably the same.

If you're me, those places are the CVS, the taco place by my house, and my own home. I make small talk with the woman who gives me my forty-five-foot-long receipt, I exchange playful glances with Esteban at the taco counter, and I spar with teens over group chat on the PlayStation Network. For me, this triangulation of human interaction is sufficient. I don't need many friends. In fact, too many human interactions per day makes me feel like a dried, discarded corn-husk doll.

But when I first moved to LA, I was pretty lonely. I consulted with Alaska Thunderfuck 5000 and she advised me to stop treating LA like a hotel room. "Does that mean you want me to stop wiping my ass on the white towels?" She said no. She said I need to MEET PEOPLE.

Hi! Hello, my name is . . . It all seems so simple. Truthfully, meeting people *is* quite easy. The challenge is being lucky enough to meet someone you'd actually like to meet with twice. I once went on a date with a guy in Milwaukee who had seemed normal enough on HelloCupid.com. He showed up, was forty pounds heavier in person, had a blue bowl cut, and literally said, "It's been a weird week since I am now off my antipsychotics." For me that was a huge red flag . . . bowl cuts were my thing.

If you do have to meet people, I advise:

Keep your hands busy! Small talk can be daunting, but when getting to know each other is built on an activity, it's much easier to stay present. When I go out, I always bring a five-gallon bucket of Atlantic surf clams. As I shuck through the shell and into the amorphous cavity, I feel much more open and in the moment. However, I am allergic to shellfish and usually need a ride to the CVS minute clinic. But even then, we are keeping our hands busy and working together. Hello there!

Wear a unique outfit! I used to love to put on a 1950s *Pleasantville* getup and stumble into a 7-Eleven acting disoriented. I'd stagger in looking confused and ask the room, "What year is it—2010? OH MY GOD I'VE BEEN ASLEEP FOR SIXTY YEARS!" If this doesn't get a reaction, you can always go back again tomorrow with a new decade look. Groovy!

Look nice. If you've read the chapters on hair and makeup, you know the transformative power of beauty. Let's be honest: People are more likely to talk to you if you are attractive. Two sponge rollers at the temple and Wispies lashes can basically get you elected to local government. If you're not attractive, then go bigger. Two powder-blue garage doors of eye shadow and a glossy lacquer of red lipstick on AND around the lips will definitely get you noticed. Just be ready to pivot the concerning glances with an attractive giggle and an inciting opener: "Well, I don't know about any of you, but I can't believe who they killed off on *American Idol* last night!"

KATYA:

If you want to fall in love or expand your group of friends, well then, I'm sorry to break it to you but you're gonna have to try to meet people. Meeting people can be a very daunting proposition, not only for the antisocial or agoraphobic, but for everyday horsies and kitties like you, my friend. Here are some ways to expand your social horizons:

Cold-calling. Pick up the phone and dial a random number. See what happens! I like to do this when I'm bored to practice my acting skills, and I've found that if you lead with "There's been a terrible accident," they tend to stay on the line.

Crying in a public place like a park or skating rink is a good way to attract new people into your life. If you're in a well-ventilated area outside, you can also nonchalantly light something on fire, perhaps your gloved hand. A little bit of drama goes a long way.

Bookstores are great places to meet people. When you spot someone who looks intriguing, ask them for the current date and time, and use that as a jumping-off point.

My number one tip for meeting new friends requires you to have a pretty significant drug or alcohol problem, or perhaps a serious food or sex addiction. Figure out which one you've got and then find a list of all the twelve-step meetings in your area, and voilà! You've now got free, unfettered access to a whole bunch of new people who are just dying to get to know you!

Of course, when it comes to romance, most people look to dating apps in order to find the one. Call me old-fashioned, but I prefer to live my life like it's a Nora Ephron movie and I'm a charming and effervescent Meg Ryan–type character who is moments away from spilling coffee on the man of my dreams. Bookstores, movie theaters, crowded delis, the post office—these are just a handful of public spaces that I barrel into with a large piping-hot cup of coffee ready to lose my balance and hurl a hot romantic splash on anyone who catches my eye.

In summary, remember: Nobody is good at talking, so just say something. If you end up saying something incredibly stupid, don't worry—most people aren't even listening.

HOOKUPS:

HOW TO HAVE SEX WITH STRANGERS

by Katya

W hen it comes to sex, I was a pretty late bloomer. Having abstained completely from sex for most of my twenties, I woke up on the eve of my thirtieth birthday feeling like I had a lot of makeup work to do. So I decided that I was going to have sex with every single man I could. And I did. That year was filled with a prodigious amount of hookups, and some weekends the frequency of sexual partners definitely hinted at a burgeoning sex addiction. But wouldn't you know it, I emerged from that year with many wonderful experiences, plenty of bad ones, and not a single sexually transmitted infection! (I already had herpes.)

Now, my situation was a bit out of the ordinary and will be relatable only to a very niche audience. That is, I'm going to assume you are probably not a thirty-year-old cross-dresser who lives alone above a drag bar. These factors came in handy when the call to hoeing rang loudly. As with most areas of life, I find it helpful to describe my pattern of behavior so that you can use it as a cautionary tale, as I am prone to living recklessly and am, by some great miracle of the Good Heavenly Lord Jesus, still alive.

Remember the Craigslist killer? Well, he should have killed me. Seriously! I met so many of my gentlemen callers on that website, often with no other background info than a badly cropped, blurry photo of them fifteen years ago. It was a nonstop cavalcade of strange men every other night of the week. The only time I didn't let a guy into my house was when he didn't show up. Looking back, I am extremely lucky that I didn't have to deal with any shenanigans of a violently physical nature at all, never mind murder.

Being as I was a very fragile and delicate woman, vulnerable to the hostile unpredictability of the outside world, I hosted my tricks 99 percent of the time. This was a much safer option than venturing into the unknown, but equally and perhaps much more important was my dignity. My particular brand of womanhood does not fare well in poorly lit environments, and my version of an overnight bag consists of two large suitcases and a Dyson vacuum cleaner. (I will not explain this.) So, it was up to me to be a gracious and sensual hostess, a role that I performed with ease and aplomb.

PLENTY OF CATFISH IN THE SEA

One of the more exciting features of hooking up in the digital age is the bait-and-switch phenomenon known as catfishing. If you've ever been on the business end of a deceiver's rod, then you'll know what a wild ride this can be. Lies, deception, stolen identities . . . it has all the soap-operatic qualities a real drama queen craves. Except the reality is just a plain old fucking bummer when you get to his house and find out that not only does he look nothing like his picture; he's not even a real person at all—just a tape-recorder shoved into a scarecrow—and now you're all alone and feeling very foolish with your pants down in the middle of a cornfield. (If I had a nickel!)

HOW TO FUCK GOOD

Here are some essential features of a good hookup, one that could lead the way to a regular fuck-buddy situation.

You're a decent host, meaning you offer water, maybe even some snacks, and you keep your living space clean and well maintained, especially the areas of immediate interest, that is, the bedroom and bathroom. I would always greet my guests at the door wearing an off-the-shoulder *Flashdance*-style sweatshirt to indicate that I am a dancer and this is a casual date. As my guest was settled into the boudoir, I would rip off the sweatshirt to reveal some very slutty high-neck, long-sleeve lingerie to let them know it was time to do sex.

You are the captain of each and every one of your sexual voyages, no matter if it's a quick slosh through the pond or a Homerian odyssey. Be clear in your objectives; be firm in what you are willing and unwilling to tolerate; and by all means, reserve the right to abandon ship at a moment's notice for any reason at any time. Listen, you are the casting director of this hookup and the policy reads: "Lineup subject to change without notice." This might involve you hopping out of the window of a horribly dull or creepy trick's bathroom when things get weird, no questions asked, no shame, and no regret. Also, it doesn't hurt to bring a knife. Well, it can definitely hurt, but that's the idea; just don't forget to stick them with the pointy end.

You take an active and determined interest in the sexual satisfaction of your partner. If you are the kind of person who collapses into the bed after you climax, while your partner's orgasm is a brief postcoital afterthought, you're an asshole. I'm looking mostly at the menfolk, though I know very well shit-heads abound in every size, color, and shape. It takes two to tango, Frank, so get back down there and make sure Vanessa isn't left high and dry. And if you can't figure out how to get things wet and wild, don't be afraid to ask the young lady what yanks her crank. A simple heartfelt query such as, "Hello, darling, I would love so much to help usher you to the absolute zenith of sexual climax. Is there anything in particular you'd like me to do that would precipitate this lovely event?" Bonus points if you're wearing a monocle and a tartan wool cape.

Allow for a reasonable postcoital buffer period, which for me can range anywhere from five to thirty minutes before I chase them out with a broom. This can be a challenge, as I have often fallen victim to a rapidly plummet-ing interest in the other person once I climax. This is why I actually, in many cases, don't care to orgasm. This sounds like a nightmare to some people, but I enjoy experiencing the other person's climax, and I am left in a state of de-sire as we part, rather than counting the minutes until this ghoulish fuckwit can put on his fucking pants and find the door. If you are the type of person who prefers a swift retreat after sex, then it's best to visit that person's house rather than having to tactfully navigate the song and dance of ejecting a now unwelcome guest.

TO TEXT OR NOT TO TEXT?

There is the three-day rule, there's the one-day rule, there's the rule of at-traction, the rule of opposites, and then there's Mercedes Ruehl. I say life is too short, so if you're thirsty, be thirsty. What's the worst that can happen? The water pitcher dries up and there's nothing to drink. Well, find another fridge. But please do take a hint. If you're going to put yourself out there, at least trade your shame in for some dignity and know when to call it quits if the other person is displaying a less-than-enthusiastic vibe about seeing you again. Think they're playing hard to get? That could be true, but guess what? I'm almost forty and I don't have time to play games, so come and get the good-good or get the hell out of my store, we're closed.

So when it comes to hooking up, remember: Sex is lovely but it isn't everything, and whether you have a shit ton or none, it's not a moral issue. It's about your physical and mental health and only you can decide if you are in balance, so don't fall prey to shady people or institutions that would slap a value judgment on you for getting your jush. Personally I don't like to be dickmatized. It's not a good look, especially since I know that a good dick is only really just that—a good dick. A great book, or a wonderful television show, or a sensationally restorative night's sleep can be equally if not more satisfying alternatives, and none of these will give you crabs.

BREAKUPS:

IT'S NOT ME, IT'S YOU

by Trixie

I knew two nonbinary lesbians who announced their breakup on Twitter. My friend, let's call her Spike, revealed that she and her partner were going through a "conscious uncoupling." Spike explained that they have mutual respect and will cherish the time that they had. She attached photos of happier times: two cropped haircuts smiling candidly. She then thanked everyone for their understanding.

I found the entire demonstration dignified, upright, and entirely bullshit.

Breakups should be met with optimism, reason, and grace. But ultimately, most of us manage uncoupling with all the confidence of a first-time liquor store robber: teeth chattering, choking on tears, and boldly trying to fire a pistol that's still on safety. As the hot salt drops stain your sun-damaged skin, you clutch a baggie of Flamin' Hot Cheetos and wonder if it was ever worth it at all.

Why do I know so much about pain? By the time I was twenty-nine, I had experienced four major breakups, each one more traumatic than the last. The important thing to remember when processing a breakup is that you are not special—breakups are part of the deal, the same way bad knees are part of high school football glory. For every intact relationship, there are two more just now expiring. For every first kiss there is a blocked phone call. And for every fateful Tinder swipe right, there is drunken breakup sex on a beanbag chair.

I dated someone long-distance for five months. He had Southern charm and owned a legion of pressed chinos. We met at a meet and greet and he said, "I'm just here with a friend; I have no idea who you are." Be still, my heart! During the next five months of barely spent time together, I proceeded to play my own personal version of Mad Libs on his personality. I sustained the weeks apart with my own trips to an imaginary lover's Build-A-Bear, fleshing him out with my own relationship ideals. What would our house look like? Would I move to the South and drink bourbon on a porch? If I suddenly went deaf, would he learn ASL for me? Would we profess our compelling love story on YouTube and would he hold me while my sponsored cochlear implant was activated? Would we be invited to *The Ellen Degeneres Show* and would she tearfully gift us MacBooks and a tote bag?

After nearly six months of intermittent honeymoons and nearly no sexual contact, the depth and breadth of his Christian guilt finally bounced me from his life like a bad check. I told him I loved him on a roller coaster in Dollywood. It was less romantic than you'd imagine: As we clicked our way to the top of the piped track, I yelled, "I LOVE YOU!" We swiftly dismounted the ride, and two weeks later, I was MTV *Next*'d.

DEVASTATED. I was wrecked. I could barely eat for months (fierce). I took up running and tanning and lost twenty-five pounds and bronzed five shades of foundation deeper. I biked the streets of Provincetown at two a.m. with a shower radio hair-tied to my handlebars. I screamed Johnny Cash B sides with a bottle of Fireball and a fistful of alarmed Tamagotchis. I also sent him a handwritten letter every day for three months. HANDWRITTEN. Even Anne Frank took a day off. Yes, I am a psychopath, and looking back, I am shocked that I was not excised from planet Earth for this *Swimfan* behavior.

Looking back, did I lose the love of my life? No. Did I lose much of anything? Girl, no. But I let this breakup be an uncontrolled test of self-indulgence. Unless your husband dies in space like Bruce Willis in *Armageddon*, you really need to calm down and assess. Is your life over? Is this anyone's fault?

No. The aftermath of shattered pieces post-breakup are actually rune stones that truth tell. If hindsight is twenty-twenty, you shouldn't feel fifty-fifty about moving on. Typically, time apart only further reveals the earliest red flags of a doomed duo.

FRIENDSHIPS:

BEST FRIENDS FOREVER

A CONVERSATION WITH TRIXIE AND KATYA

KATYA: So, do adults have best friends?

TRIXIE: Don't you think that when you're in sixth grade, "best friend" is like a hierarchy of who's your ride or die? And it's sort of like the Myspace Top 8?

T: Now I don't think people have best friends, because things like distance and frequency of how much you see each other don't really mean that person's your best friend. When you have a normal job, like, a nine-to-five, you might have your work best friend. That's your work friend. And then your boyfriend or husband or wife is arguably your best friend. A lot of people say that's their best friend.

K: Some people do maintain relationships from elementary school, I've been told, into their adult years. But I feel like the term "best friend," when you're past thirty, is a little juvenile.

T: Yes! I have one friend, we've been close best friends probably since fourth grade. But we don't see each other very often, but I would still say because of the span of years, she is one of my closest friends. But best friend? Maybe I'm fickle. Somebody is my best friend one second and I don't want to see them the next second. I think it's a red flag when someone as an adult is like, "That's my best friend."

K: I immediately think of needy, immature, and perhaps manipulative?

T: "My best friend. You're my best friend."

K: Yeah. Ginger Minj.

T: Did you say Ginger Minj? Oh shit! Let the record show that she said . . . Well, here's the thing about best friends. Sometimes it's really just a one-way street. You know what I mean? There's somebody in our lives who is like "I'm coming over." And I'm like, my own boyfriend doesn't tell me, "I'm coming over."

K: Back off, Mary.

T: And if you wanna be my best friend, you got to know that I might want to see you once every two weeks. That's the closeness I need. When I was younger I was much more like, "Who's going out tonight? What's going on? I got to see someone." I was, like, always wanting to fill my free time with social things. And now I'm like . . . Maybe it's because of drag. It's like when you snatch the wig off and sit in the dark.

K: I was never like that when I was younger. But I think you said it before, too, especially performing, doing gigs, is such a unique and intense expenditure of social energy.

T: And very fulfilling.

K: Oh, absolutely! But it's draining. You're addressing a thousand people for a whole night! You're just like, "UH! Get away from me," afterward. Makes sense that you need a lot of time to recharge. I felt that.

T: Okay, this is not related. Boundaries. When you and me and Courtney Act were in Boston at an outdoor café and this fan walked up and sat down at our table and you went, "Oh no, you can't sit down."

K: Yeah, yeah. I was so proud of myself. Because in those situations you gotta nip it right in the bud. You've got to establish the boundary. And normally I wouldn't be able to do that, and then we would have been stuck with her the whole night. She would have slept over at my house.

T: Work.

K: Anyway, back to best friends. I was always the person who was everybody's best friend, but I never had a best friend. Do you know what I mean? At any given time, six to eight people would call me their best friend, and I'm like, "I don't know who they are."

T: I do think that, because of your personality, you do have quite a charisma to you, and it is fleeting. In the sense of, like, you're actually fleeing the room. "She was nice. Is she coming back in here?" "She went home." "Oh, she didn't say bye to anybody." "Yeah, she just left."

K: Back to best friends for a minute. Ride or die? What are we riding and how are we dying? Like, what does that expression really mean? Is this like ride and die? Like *Thelma and Louise*?

T: Well, doesn't that mean that, like, that's your person, it means that person sticks with you no matter what. I only say that about makeup products. I'm like, mama, Maybelline SuperStay is my ride or die. But my husband . . .

K: Fuck him.

T: Listen, I might be damaged, my man might leave me, my production company might cancel me, I might get fired, my Uber might report me, but mama that MAC Edge to Edge lip liner has me boots.

K: But is there anybody you would break the law with? Or cover up a crime for, or perjure on the stand for? Things of that nature.

T: Well, are you familiar with the program—this might be a little too real for you—but it's called *Breaking Bad*?

K: Oh yeah, yeah, yeah.

T: She finds out that her husband is making meth. And she is mad. And then she's like, "Well, you're my ride or die. Like, if you're doing this, I'm going to help you do it right." Because she's an accountant, I believe.

K: Skyler?

T: Yeah, she's like, "I gotta cook your books for you or you're gonna get caught." That is an example of a ride-or-die relationship. That is an example of when ride or die is the wrong thing. Because I have friends who I'm ride or die for, but I'm like, I'm not willing to die for you.

K: Right. Would you die for anybody? Would you die for love?

T: I have younger siblings. I'd probably die for them.

K: Yeah. I'd die for my sister.

T: You have a younger sister, right? So then there's like a blood bond. There's a snap judgment of, like, "Oh yeah, I'd take a bullet for them." But my older brother, probably not.

K: I would also die for my older brother. He's got a kid.

T: And honestly, you're on borrowed time anyway.

K: I've had enough.

T: Enough, sis!

TRIXIE: We need to change that expression to: "You're my ride and die."

KATYA: Cruise and lose.

TRIXIE: We're gonna go for a ride—

KATYA: And we're gonna die.

T: Oh, would you ever have a threesome with someone who's your friend? Have you ever slept with a friend? Most of my people I've slept with, I slept with them so early on in our friendship that I completely forgot we ever did. Or I had a crush on them at one point and then the friendship sort of dissolves it.

K: Oh yeah, actually, there was a point where every straight male friend I had, I was in love with for at least three months. And then I just got over it.

T: I do think that's very typical gay man, though. You fall in love with the one who's not going to love you back because it's safer than mutual intimacy.

K: Yeah, it's safer than intimacy and then you won't be rejected because you'll never be accepted.

T: Because you'll never be accepted. Gag.

K: So no, I haven't fucked friends.

T: I've fucked friends. I have friends that maybe I met because I was attracted to them or we slept together once and then it's like . . . we stay friends because we like each other as friends but we're not attracted anymore. I think that's probably more common in the gay world.
Don't you think gay groups are very incestuous, like everyone's fucked everyone?

K: I get the sense when I meet, especially the white gays . . . They're like the show *Friends*. They've all fucked each other. Even the sisters. Not the sisters, but they all fuck each other.

T: *Sister Act*? Whoopie was fucking the nuns in *Sister Act*?

K: In *Friends*, the show *Friends*. Are any of them brother and sister? Ross and Monica are sister and brother?

T: I think that might be true. I've never seen it.

K: It's . . . not good.

T: Well, why do people nut for it, then? It's a show about friends.

K: It's not remarkable. It's not that great. It kind of sucks. Doesn't matter.

T: And that haircut. The Rachel.

K: Mama. Cultural impact.

T: If you want to read about the Rachel, see page 13.

K: Yeah. So what does your friend group look like?

T: Is it sad if I don't have a lot of friends?

K: No. It's only sad if you're sad that you don't have a lot of friends.

T: I'm not, because the friends I have are enough and close enough connections. I don't see Fena every day, but I could call her out of the blue and be like, "You wanna kiki?" Good friends are when you don't need to see each other; it's not about constant upkeep.

K: You pick up right where you left off.

T: You know what our friendship thrives on? We don't need to see each other. I like to kiki with you. I probably call or text you more than other people. Half the time it's work related. We're lucky because our friendship lives in a frame where we actually have shit to do. It's admittedly much harder to maintain friendships when there's not some life circumstance drawing you together.

K: I agree.

T: Which is why work friends . . .

K: And neighbors, yeah.

T: Is it sad that because I see my personal trainer so much I'm like, I guess he's one of my close friends now. But we have an agenda so we can really relax. If you are friends with the people you work with, you don't need to go home and seek out a social experience. You are a sim and your social meter got filled up while you were at work and that's fine.

K: At the gym!

T: Retail? When I worked at MAC and I would go home, and people were like, "We're going out," and I'm like, I can't talk to anybody else.

K: That is a lot of social engagement.

T: And it's performing. Retail is performing. You have to create a persona.

K: Yeah, you have to really lay it on thick. Especially if you're an aggressive salesperson and you have quotas to fill.

T: The whole script of, like, "Hi, welcome! Oh, I love that shirt. What do you wanna play with today? What are you looking for? What you wanna work on?" However, it works because we have something to do. Having a common struggle sometimes forges great friendships because you're the most yourself.

K: Yeah.

T: Because you have something to do. That make sense?

K: No. Explain.

T: When you're on a date and you're just sitting there staring at each other. It's weird to actually be yourself. Versus, like . . .

K: An activity! Jumping out of a plane.

T: Hiding a body.

K: Oh, how about this one: cutting people loose. Toxic people. Do you get into the expression "toxic people"? I think it's a red flag. For the people who say that.

T: I agree. I don't think I've ever cut people loose, but sometimes I have . . .

K: Let them fade away.

T: Yeah, you begin to notice something in them that you didn't see initially. They come into focus the more you get to know someone . . . It's sorta like dating. Where you go, "Oh, now that it's a clearer picture of you . . ."

K: "Oh, you're shitty."

T: "This is our friendship's depth and I don't wanna go deeper." We know a drag queen who consciously cut me loose and that was it. No talking anymore. Some people do that but I don't think it's unhealthy.

K: I think it's crazy. When I was actively psychotic, I remember thinking a lot along those terms, but that's insane thinking to me.

T: It says more about the person.

K: Absolutely, I think it gives you all you need to know about that person and that person only.

T: This year, no more toxic energy, no more drama.

K: Anybody who says, "I'm over the bullshit, I'm over the drama . . ."

T: They *are* the bullshit and they *are* the drama!

K: Yes, they are! It's so ridiculous. *Drag Race* is a good example of friendship by fire and then friendship by choice. Because once you get out of there, you're like, "Oh, I don't know if I really like these people."

T: Yeah, sometimes you get out of there and everything is clear in hindsight. You're like, "Whoa!" Like one of my friendships in high school. We were close, but maybe we were close out of necessity. Maybe that was just the most compatible person I could find.

K: Yeah. There was one person from *Drag Race* I went and visited shortly after the season and I was like, "Oh no, this is rotten."

T: It's different in the wild.

K: It was like the lights were on and it smelled like whodunnit.

T: But you know what, that's the part of getting to know people. That's why getting to know people is exhausting, because it's rarely a returning investment.

K: I've always had this problem where none of my friends get along with each other. I found myself in the situation where I hang out with one or two people at a time but never a large group, and if I put all these people in a group it would be chaos. And then I'm like, "Am I a sociopath 'cause I'm a different person with each one of these people?"

T: Oh, you actually change with them. Well, that's not true. Each one of their personalities bring out different parts of you.

K: OOOOOH! So have you ever had a friend turn on you . . . Well, yes, you have, but, HEHE.

T: HAHAHA girl, let me tell you a story. The year was 2018 . . . (see chapter titled "Pills, Pipes, and Potions").

K: Listen to this. So, I had these two friends when I was a kid, Stuart and Dennis. So, they both *turned* . . . They turned for the worse. We were all really close friends since two years old. As we went to college, Dennis became a fuckin' born-again Christian, and then Stuart, who had been weird and alternative like me, became a complete MassHole. Like, if I came in here and started talking like fuckin' Good Will Hunting.

T: Stepford wives of eastern Massachusetts.

K: That's what Stuart did, overnight. Then Dennis wrote me a fucking handwritten letter inviting me to join him in defeating the forces of evil for God, and then he died. He got murdered. Hello!

T: I get so scared because I feel like everyone in your stories ends up getting murdered. You're always the common thread.

K: What's even weirder than murder is when you look him in the face and think, "You are not the same person and you haven't been lobotomized." But it seems like it! Like totally lobotomized, like you've regressed.

T: Well . . . people change a lot at that time. I bet you Stuart left high school–joined the workforce somewhere. His work friends became his friends, and then you assimilate.

K: He dropped out of college, got fat, became a plumber, got some girl knocked up, he's a dad now. He literally became his dad. I mean, good for him I guess, but to me it was so strange.

T: Well, the friendships you have definitely influence your package deal. People bounce their shit off of you and you keep things. My sister has braids.

K: She got cornrows.

T: Cornrows.

K: White girl.

T: Cornrows! I said we are from Wisconsin. But cornrows . . .

K: Does she listen to gangster rap?

T: Yes, and vapes and has neck tattoos.

K: Does she do lean?

T: I don't think so.

K: Okay. She should get into Ensure.

T: But, like, my sister was a country girl from the country and then she moved to the city for beauty school.

K: She *turned.*

T: Her entire music taste, personal style. But then again, she's eighteen, nineteen, twenty. That's the time in your life when people come in and shape you.

K: I was in Tennessee for forty-eight hours and I left with an accent. I swear to God.

T: Work. This happened in high school. This girl I went to France with, she started to talk in a fake French accent, and I was like . . . Who are you??

K: You are American. You're [CLAP] American [CLAP].

T: It was a week in France and she was already on that.

K: Yeah, that's totally me.

"KATYA: Do you think the friends you have now you'll keep for a good long time, until you're dead?

TRIXIE: Well, umm . . .

KATYA: Are you accepting applications?"

T: People come into your life for a reason, a season, or a lifetime . . . I have that painted on my wall. Would you talk to me if it said, like, "Family," on that wall?

K: I would if it said, "Take a shit in the corner."

T: Like, "Joy is just smiling." I don't know, whatever. "Dance like no one is booing." That's what I want on the wall.

K: HAHA. Dance like no one is giving you the finger.

T: Breathe like no one's farted.

K: Anyway. Are you a Carrie, Samantha, or Charlotte?

T: I'm a Darien. Is that one of them? Rudolph.

K: Monica, Phoebe, or a Rachel? Are you a Mary-Kate or Ashley?

T: Here's a good closer question. What do you seek from a friendship personally? 'Cause I think everyone is in it for something different. I'm very attracted to friends that have their own shit and their own hustle. I actually like to think in my friendships; I try to be more of the listener. We talk so much about ourselves in the world. Somebody interesting where I can be like, "What are you making? Tell me all about it."

K: Yeah. Tell me every little thing about it.

T: I have a friend who is a scientist and I'm like, "What are you doing at work? You did what?"

K: Yeah! Or somebody who works at an office. Who's the bitch? What's in the break-room fridge? What's the hierarchy like? It's fascinating.